**Hard Press**

THE HOPE OF THE GOSPEL

BY

GEORGE MACDONALD

# Contents

SALVATION FROM SIN

THE REMISSION OF SINS

JESUS IN THE WORLD

JESUS AND HIS FELLOW TOWNSMEN

THE HEIRS OF HEAVEN AND EARTH

SORROW THE PLEDGE OF JOY

GOD'S FAMILY

THE REWARD OF OBEDIENCE

THE YOKE OF JESUS

THE SALT AND THE LIGHT OF THE WORLD

THE RIGHT HAND AND THE LEFT

# THE HOPE OF THE UNIVERSE

*SALVATION FROM SIN.*

—and thou shalt call his name Jesus; for he shall save his people from their sins.—*Matthew* i. 21.

I would help some to understand what Jesus came from the home of our Father to be to us and do for us. Everything in the world is more or less misunderstood at first: we have to learn what it is, and come at length to see that it must be so, that it could not be otherwise. Then we know it; and we never know a thing *really* until we know it thus.

I presume there is scarce a human being who, resolved to speak openly, would not confess to having something that plagued him, something from which he would gladly be free, something rendering it impossible for him, at the moment, to regard life as an altogether good thing. Most men, I presume, imagine that, free of such and such things antagonistic, life would be an unmingled satisfaction, worthy of being prolonged indefinitely. The causes of their discomfort are of all kinds, and the degrees of it reach from simple uneasiness to a misery such as makes annihilation the highest hope of the sufferer who can persuade himself of its possibility. Perhaps the greater part of the energy of this world's life goes forth in the endeavour to rid itself of discomfort. Some, to escape it, leave their natural surroundings behind them, and with strong and continuous effort keep rising in the social scale, to discover at every new ascent fresh trouble, as they think, awaiting them, whereas in truth they have brought the trouble with them. Others, making haste to be rich, are slow to find out that the poverty of their souls, none the less that their purses are filling, will yet keep them unhappy. Some court endless change, nor know that on themselves the change must pass that will set them free. Others expand their souls with knowledge, only to find that content will not dwell in the great house they have built. To number the varieties of human endeavour to escape discomfort would be to enumerate all the modes of such life as does not know how to live. All seek the thing whose defect appears the *cause* of their misery, and is but the variable *occasion* of it, the cause of the shape it takes, not of the misery itself; for, when one apparent cause is removed, another at once succeeds. The real cause of his trouble is a something the man has not perhaps recognized as even existent; in any case he is not yet acquainted with its true nature.

However absurd the statement may appear to one who has not yet discovered the fact for himself, the cause of every man's discomfort is evil, moral evil—first of all, evil in himself, his own sin, his own wrongness, his own unrightness; and then, evil in those he loves: with this latter I have not now to deal; the only way to get rid of it, is for the man to get rid of his own sin. No special sin may be recognizable as having caused this or that special physical discomfort—which may indeed have originated with some ancestor; but evil in ourselves is the cause of its continuance, the source of its necessity, and the preventive of that patience which would soon take from it, or at least blunt its sting. The evil is *essentially* unnecessary, and passes with the attainment of the object for which it is permitted—namely, the development of pure will in man; the suffering also is essentially unnecessary, but while the evil lasts, the suffering, whether consequent or merely concomitant, is absolutely necessary. Foolish is the man, and there are many such men, who would rid himself or his fellows of discomfort by setting the world right, by waging war on the evils around him, while he neglects that integral part of the world where lies his business, his first business—namely, his own character and conduct. Were it possible—an absurd supposition—that the world should thus be righted from the outside, it would yet be impossible for the man who had contributed to the work, remaining what he was, ever to enjoy the perfection of the result; himself not in tune with the organ he had tuned, he must imagine it still a distracted, jarring instrument. The philanthropist who regards the wrong as in the race, forgetting that the race is made up of conscious and wrong individuals, forgets also that wrong is always generated in and done by an individual; that the wrongness exists in the individual, and by him is passed over, as tendency, to the race; and that no evil can be cured in the race, except by its being cured in its individuals: tendency is not absolute evil; it is there that it may be resisted, not yielded to. There is no way of making three men right but by making right each one of the three; but a cure in one man who repents and turns, is a beginning of the cure of the whole human race.

Even if a man's suffering be a far inheritance, for the curing of which by faith and obedience this life would not be sufficiently long, faith and obedience will yet render it endurable to the man, and overflow in help to his fellow-sufferers. The groaning body, wrapt in the garment of hope, will, with outstretched neck, look for its redemption, and endure.

The one cure for any organism, is to be set right—to have all its parts brought into harmony with each other; the one comfort is to know this cure in process. Rightness alone is cure. The return of the organism to its true self, is its only possible ease. To free a man from suffering, he must be set right, put in health; and the health at the root of man's being, his rightness, is to be free from wrongness, that is, from sin. A man is right when there is no wrong in him. The wrong, the evil is in him; he must be set free from it. I do not mean set free from the sins he has done: that will follow; I mean the sins he is doing, or is capable of doing; the sins in his being which spoil his nature—the wrongness in him—the evil he consents to; the sin he is, which makes him do the sin he does.

To save a man from his sins, is to say to him, in sense perfect and eternal, 'Rise up and walk. Be at liberty in thy essential being. Be free as the son of God is free.' To do this for us, Jesus was born, and remains born to all the ages. When misery drives a man to call out to the source of his life,—and I take the increasing outcry against existence as a sign of the growth of the race toward a sense of the need of regeneration—the answer, I think, will come in a quickening of his conscience. This earnest of the promised deliverance may not, in all probability will not be what the man desires; he will want only to be rid of his suffering; but that he cannot have, save in being delivered from its essential root, a thing infinitely worse than any suffering it can produce. If he will not have that deliverance, he must keep his suffering. Through chastisement he will take at last the only way that leads into the liberty of that which is and must be. There can be no deliverance but to come out of his evil dream into the glory of God.

It is true that Jesus came, in delivering us from our sins, to deliver us also from the painful consequences of our sins. But these consequences exist by the one law of the universe, the true will of the Perfect. That broken, that disobeyed by the creature, disorganization renders suffering inevitable; it is the natural consequence of the unnatural—and, in the perfection of God's creation, the result is curative of the cause; the pain at least tends to the healing of the breach. The Lord never came to deliver men from the consequences of their sins while yet those sins remained: that would be to cast out of window the medicine of cure while yet the man lay sick; to go dead against the very laws of being. Yet men, loving their sins, and feeling nothing of their dread hatefulness, have, consistently with their low condition, constantly taken this word concerning the Lord to mean that he came to save them from the punishment of their sins. The idea—the miserable fancy rather—has terribly corrupted the preaching of the gospel. The message of the good news has not been truly delivered. Unable to believe in the forgiveness of their Father in heaven, imagining him not at liberty to forgive, or incapable of forgiving forthright; not really believing him God our Saviour, but a God bound, either in his own nature or by a law above him and compulsory upon him, to exact some recompense or satisfaction for sin, a multitude of teaching men have taught their fellows that Jesus came to bear our punishment and save us from hell. They have represented a result as the object of his mission—the said result nowise to be desired by true man save as consequent on the gain of his object. The mission of Jesus was from the same source and with the same object as the punishment of our sins. He came to work along with our punishment. He came to side with it, and set us free from our sins. No man is safe from hell until he is free from his sins; but a man to whom his sins, that is the evil things in him, are a burden, while he may indeed sometimes feel as if he were in hell, will soon have forgotten that ever he had any other hell to think of than that of his sinful condition. For to him his sins are hell; he would go to the other hell to be free of them; free of them, hell itself would be endurable to him. For hell is God's and not the devil's. Hell is on the side of God and man, to free the child of God from the corruption of death. Not one soul will ever be redeemed from hell but by being saved from his sins, from the evil in him. If hell be needful to save him, hell will blaze, and the worm will writhe and bite, until he takes refuge in the will of the Father. 'Salvation from hell, is salvation as conceived by such to whom hell and not evil is the terror.' But if even for dread of hell a poor soul seek the Father, he will be heard of him in his terror, and, taught of him to seek the immeasurably greater gift, will in the greater receive the less.

There is another important misapprehension of the words of the messengers of the good tidings—that they threaten us with punishment because of the sins we have committed, whereas their message is of forgiveness, not of vengeance; of deliverance, not of evil to come. Not for anything he has committed do they threaten a man with the outer darkness. Not for any or all of his sins that are past shall a man be condemned; not for the worst of them needs he dread remaining unforgiven. The sin he dwells in, the sin he will not come out of, is the sole ruin of a man. His

7

present, his live sins—those pervading his thoughts and ruling his conduct; the sins he keeps doing, and will not give up; the sins he is called to abandon, and clings to; the same sins which are the cause of his misery, though he may not know it—these are they for which he is even now condemned. It is true the memory of the wrongs we have done is, or will become very bitter; but not for those is condemnation; and if that in our character which made them possible were abolished, remorse would lose its worst bitterness in the hope of future amends. 'This is the condemnation, that light is come into the world, and men loved darkness rather than light, because their deeds were evil.'

It is the indwelling badness, ready to produce bad actions, that we need to be delivered from. Against this badness if a man will not strive, he is left to commit evil and reap the consequences. To be saved from these consequences, would be no deliverance; it would be an immediate, ever deepening damnation. It is the evil in our being—no essential part of it, thank God!—the miserable fact that the very child of God does not care for his father and will not obey him, causing us to desire wrongly, act wrongly, or, where we try not to act wrongly, yet making it impossible for us not to feel wrongly—this is what he came to deliver us from;—not the things we have done, but the possibility of doing such things any more. With the departure of this possibility, and with the hope of confession hereafter to those we have wronged, will depart also the power over us of the evil things we have done, and so we shall be saved from them also. The bad that lives in us, our evil judgments, our unjust desires, our hate and pride and envy and greed and self-satisfaction—these are the souls of our sins, our live sins, more terrible than the bodies of our sins, namely the deeds we do, inasmuch as they not only produce these loathsome things, but make us loathsome as they. Our wrong deeds are our dead works; our evil thoughts are our live sins. These, the essential opposites of faith and love, the sins that dwell and work in us, are the sins from which Jesus came to deliver us. When we turn against them and refuse to obey them, they rise in fierce insistence, but the same moment begin to die. We are then on the Lord's side, as he has always been on ours, and he begins to deliver us from them.

Anything in you, which, in your own child, would make you feel him not so pleasant as you would have him, is something wrong. This may mean much to one, little or nothing to another. Things in a child which to one parent would not seem worth minding, would fill another with horror. After his moral development, where the one parent would smile, the other would look aghast, perceiving both the present evil, and the serpent-brood to follow. But as the love of him who is love, transcends ours as the heavens are higher than the earth, so must he desire in his child infinitely more than the most jealous love of the best mother can desire in hers. He would have him rid of all discontent, all fear, all grudging, all bitterness in word or thought, all gauging and measuring of his own with a different rod from that he would apply to another's. He will have no curling of the lip; no indifference in him to the man whose service in any form he uses; no desire to excel another, no contentment at gaining by his loss. He will not have him receive the smallest service without gratitude; would not hear from him a tone to jar the heart of another, a word to make it ache, be the ache ever so transient. From such, as from all other sins, Jesus was born to deliver us; not, primarily, or by itself, from the punishment of any of them.

When all are gone, the holy punishment will have departed also. He came to make us good, and therein blessed children.

One master-sin is at the root of all the rest. It is no individual action, or anything that comes of mood, or passion; it is the non-recognition by the man, and consequent inactivity in him, of the highest of all relations, that relation which is the root and first essential condition of every other true relation of or in the human soul. It is the absence in the man of harmony with the being whose thought is the man's existence, whose word is the man's power of thought. It is true that, being thus his offspring, God, as St Paul affirms, cannot be far from any one of us: were we not in closest contact of creating and created, we could not exist; as we have in us no power to be, so have we none to continue being; but there is a closer contact still, as absolutely necessary to our well-being and highest existence, as the other to our being at all, to the mere capacity of faring well or ill. For the highest creation of God in man is his will, and until the highest in man meets the highest in God, their true relation is not yet a spiritual fact. The flower lies in the root, but the root is not the flower. The relation exists, but while one of the parties neither knows, loves, nor acts upon it, the relation is, as it were, yet unborn. The highest in man is neither his intellect nor his imagination nor his reason; all are inferior to his will, and indeed, in a grand way, dependent upon it: his will must meet God's—a will *distinct* from God's, else were no *harmony* possible between them. Not the less, therefore, but the more, is all God's. For God creates in the man the power to will His will. It may cost God a suffering man can never know, to bring the man to the point at which he will will His will; but when he is brought to that point, and declares for the truth, that is, for the will of God, he becomes one with God, and the end of God in the man's creation, the end for which Jesus was born and died, is gained. The man is saved from his sins, and the universe flowers yet again in his redemption. But I would not be supposed, from what I have said, to imagine the Lord without sympathy for the sorrows and pains which reveal what sin is, and by means of which he would make men sick of sin. With everything human he sympathizes. Evil is not human; it is the defect and opposite of the human; but the suffering that follows it is human, belonging of necessity to the human that has sinned: while it is by cause of sin, suffering is *for* the sinner, that he may be delivered from his sin. Jesus is in himself aware of every human pain. He feels it also. In him too it is pain. With the energy of tenderest love he wills his brothers and sisters free, that he may fill them to overflowing with that essential thing, joy. For that they were indeed created. But the moment they exist, truth becomes the first thing, not happiness; and he must make them true. Were it possible, however, for pain to continue after evil was gone, he would never rest while one ache was yet in the world. Perfect in sympathy, he feels in himself, I say, the tortured presence of every nerve that lacks its repose. The man may recognize the evil in him only as pain; he may know little and care nothing about his sins; yet is the Lord sorry for his pain. He cries aloud, 'Come unto me, all ye that labour and are heavy laden, and I will give you rest.' He does not say, 'Come unto me, all ye that feel the burden of your sins;' he opens his arms to all weary enough to come to him in the poorest hope of rest. Right gladly would he free them from their misery—but he knows only one way: he will teach them to be like himself, meek and lowly, bearing with gladness the yoke of his father's will. This is the one, the only right, the only possible way of freeing them from their sins, the cause of their unrest. With

9

them the weariness comes first; with him the sins: there is but one cure for both—the will of the Father. That which is his joy will be their deliverance! He might indeed, it may be, take from them the human, send them down to some lower stage of being, and so free them from suffering—but that must be either a descent toward annihilation, or a fresh beginning to grow up again toward the region of suffering they have left; for that which is not growing must at length die out of creation. The disobedient and selfish would fain in the hell of their hearts possess the liberty and gladness that belong to purity and love, but they cannot have them; they are weary and heavy-laden, both with what they are, and because of what they were made for but are not. The Lord knows what they need; they know only what they want. They want ease; he knows they need purity. Their very existence is an evil, of which, but for his resolve to purify them, their maker must rid his universe. How can he keep in his sight a foul presence? Must the creator send forth his virtue to hold alive a thing that will be evil—a thing that ought not to be, that has no claim but to cease? The Lord himself would not live save with an existence absolutely good.

It may be my reader will desire me to say *how* the Lord will deliver him from his sins. That is like the lawyer's 'Who is my neighbour?' The spirit of such a mode of receiving the offer of the Lord's deliverance, is the root of all the horrors of a corrupt theology, so acceptable to those who love weak and beggarly hornbooks of religion. Such questions spring from the passion for the fruit of the tree of knowledge, not the fruit of the tree of life. Men would understand: they do not care to *obey*,—understand where it is impossible they should understand save by obeying. They would search into the work of the Lord instead of doing their part in it—thus making it impossible both for the Lord to go on with his work, and for themselves to become capable of seeing and understanding what he does. Instead of immediately obeying the Lord of life, the one condition upon which he can help them, and in itself the beginning of their deliverance, they set themselves to question their unenlightened intellects as to his plans for their deliverance—and not merely how he means to effect it, but how he can be able to effect it. They would bind their Samson until they have scanned his limbs and thews. Incapable of understanding the first motions of freedom in themselves, they proceed to interpret the riches of his divine soul in terms of their own beggarly notions, to paraphrase his glorious verse into their own paltry commercial prose; and then, in the growing presumption of imagined success, to insist upon their neighbours' acceptance of their distorted shadows of 'the plan of salvation' as the truth of him in whom is no darkness, and the one condition of their acceptance with him. They delay setting their foot on the stair which alone can lead them to the house of wisdom, until they shall have determined the material and mode of its construction. For the sake of knowing, they postpone that which alone can enable them to know, and substitute for the true understanding which lies beyond, a false persuasion that they already understand. They will not accept, that is, act upon, their highest privilege, that of obeying the Son of God. It is on them that do his will, that the day dawns; to them the day-star arises in their hearts. Obedience is the soul of knowledge.

By obedience, I intend no kind of obedience to man, or submission to authority claimed by man or community of men. I mean obedience to the will of the Father, however revealed in our conscience.

God forbid I should seem to despise understanding. The New Testament is full of urgings to understand. Our whole life, to be life at all, must be a growth in understanding. What I cry out upon is the misunderstanding that comes of man's endeavour to understand while not obeying. Upon obedience our energy must be spent; understanding will follow. Not anxious to know our duty, or knowing it and not doing it, how shall we understand that which only a true heart and a clean soul can ever understand? The power in us that would understand were it free, lies in the bonds of imperfection and impurity, and is therefore incapable of judging the divine. It cannot see the truth. If it could see it, it would not know it, and would not have it. Until a man begins to obey, the light that is in him is darkness.

Any honest soul may understand this much, however—for it is a thing we may of ourselves judge to be right—that the Lord cannot save a man from his sins while he holds to his sins. An omnipotence that could do and not do the same thing at the same moment, were an idea too absurd for mockery; an omnipotence that could at once make a man a free man, and leave him a self-degraded slave—make him the very likeness of God, and good only because he could not help being good, would be an idea of the same character—equally absurd, equally self-contradictory.

But the Lord is not unreasonable; he requires no high motives where such could not yet exist. He does not say, 'You must be sorry for your sins, or you need not come to me:' to be sorry for his sins a man must love God and man, and love is the very thing that has to be developed in him. It is but common sense that a man, longing to be freed from suffering, or made able to bear it, should betake himself to the Power by whom he is. Equally is it common sense that, if a man would be delivered from the evil in him, he must himself begin to cast it out, himself begin to disobey it, and work righteousness. As much as either is it common sense that a man should look for and expect the help of his Father in the endeavour. Alone, he might labour to all eternity and not succeed. He who has not made himself, cannot set himself right without him who made him. But his maker is in him, and is his strength. The man, however, who, instead of doing what he is told, broods speculating on the metaphysics of him who calls him to his work, stands leaning his back against the door by which the Lord would enter to help him. The moment he sets about putting straight the thing that is crooked—I mean doing right where he has been doing wrong, he withdraws from the entrance, gives way for the Master to come in. He cannot make himself pure, but he can leave that which is impure; he can spread out the 'defiled, discoloured web' of his life before the bleaching sun of righteousness; he cannot save himself, but he can let the Lord save him. The struggle of his weakness is as essential to the coming victory as the strength of Him who resisted unto death, striving against sin.

The sum of the whole matter is this:—The Son has come from the Father to set the children free from their sins; the children must hear and obey him, that he may send forth judgment unto victory.

Son of our Father, help us to do what thou sayest, and so with thee die unto sin, that we may rise to the sonship for which we were created. Help us to repent even to the sending away of our sins.

## THE REMISSION OF SINS.

John did baptize in the wilderness, and preach the baptism of repentance for the remission of sins.—*Mark* i. 4.

God and man must combine for salvation from sin, and the same word, here and elsewhere translated *remission*, seems to be employed in the New Testament for the share of either in the great deliverance.

But first let me say something concerning the word here and everywhere translated *repentance*. I would not even suggest a mistranslation; but the idea intended by the word has been so misunderstood and therefore mistaught, that it requires some consideration of the word itself to get at a right recognition of the moral fact it represents.

The Greek word then, of which the word *repentance* is the accepted synonym and fundamentally the accurate rendering, is made up of two words, the conjoint meaning of which is, *a change of mind* or *thought*. There is in it no intent of, or hint at *sorrow* or *shame*, or any other of the mental conditions that, not unfrequently accompanying repentance, have been taken for essential parts of it, sometimes for its very essence. Here, the last of the prophets, or the evangelist who records his doings, qualifies the word, as if he held it insufficient in itself to convey the Baptist's meaning, with the three words that follow it—*[Greek: eis aPhesin amartion:— kaerusson Baptisma metauoias eis aphesin amartion]*—'preaching a baptism of repentance—*unto a sending away of sins'*. I do not say the phrase *[Greek: aphesis amartion]* never means *forgiveness,* one form at least of *God's* sending away of sins; neither do I say that the taking of the phrase to mean *repentance for the remission of sins,* namely, repentance in order to obtain the pardon of God, involves any inconsistency; but I say that the word *[Greek: eis]* rather *unto* than *for;* that the word *[Greek: aphesis],* translated *remission,* means, fundamentally, a *sending away,* a *dismissal;* and that the writer seems to use the added phrase to make certain what he means by *repentance;* a repentance, namely, that reaches to the sending away, or abjurement of sins. I do not think *a change of mind unto the remission or pardon of sin* would be nearly so logical a phrase as *a change of mind unto the dismission of sinning.* The revised version refuses the word *for* and chooses *unto,* though it retains *remission,* which word, now, conveys no meaning except the forgiveness of God. I think that here the same word is used for man's dismission of his sins, as is elsewhere used for God's dismission or remission of them. In both uses, it is a sending away of sins, with the difference of meaning that comes from the differing sources of the action. Both God and man send away sins, but in the one case God sends away the sins of the man, and in the other the man sends away his own sins. I do not enter into the question whether God's aphesis may or may not mean as well the sending of his sins out of a man, as the pardon of them; whether it may not sometimes mean *dismission,* and sometimes *remission*: I am sure the one deed cannot be separated from the other.

That the phrase here intends repentance unto the ceasing from sin, the giving up of what is wrong, I will try to show at least probable.

In the first place, the user of the phrase either defines the change of mind he means as one that has for its object the pardon of God, or as one that reaches to a new life: the latter seems to me the more natural interpretation by far. The kind and scope of the repentance or change, and not any end to be gained by it, appears intended. The change must be one of will and conduct—a radical change of life on the part of the man: he must repent—that is, change his mind—not to a different opinion, not even to a mere betterment of his conduct—not to anything less than a sending away of his sins. This interpretation of the preaching of the Baptist seems to me, I repeat, the more direct, the fuller of meaning, the more logical.

Next, in St Matthew's gospel, the Baptist's buttressing argument, or imminent motive for the change he is pressing upon the people is, that the kingdom of heaven is at hand: 'Because the king of heaven is coming, you must give up your sinning.' The same argument for immediate action lies in his quotation from Isaiah,—'Prepare ye the way of the Lord; make straight in the desert a highway for our God.' The only true, the only possible preparation for the coming Lord, is to cease from doing evil, and begin to do well—to send away sin. They must cleanse, not the streets of their cities, not their houses or their garments or even their persons, but their hearts and their doings. It is true the Baptist did not see that the kingdom coming was not of this world, but of the higher world in the hearts of men; it is true that his faith failed him in his imprisonment, because he heard of no martial movement on the part of the Lord, no assertion of his sovereignty, no convincing show of his power; but he did see plainly that righteousness was essential to the kingdom of heaven. That he did not yet perceive that righteousness *is* the kingdom of heaven; that he did not see that the Lord was already initiating his kingdom by sending away sin out of the hearts of his people, is not wonderful. The Lord's answer to his fore-runner's message of doubt, was to send his messenger back an eye-witness of what he was doing, so to wake or clarify in him the perception that his kingdom was not of this world—that he dealt with other means to another end than John had yet recognized as his mission or object; for obedient love in the heart of the poorest he healed or persuaded, was his kingdom come.

Again, observe that, when the Pharisees came to John, he said to them, 'Bring forth therefore fruits meet for repentance:' is not this the same as, 'Repent unto the sending away of your sins'?

Note also, that, when the multitudes came to the prophet, and all, with the classes most obnoxious to the rest, the publicans and the soldiers, asked what he would have them do—thus plainly recognizing that something was required of them—his instruction was throughout in the same direction: they must send away their sins; and each must begin with the fault that lay next him. The kingdom of heaven was at hand: they must prepare the way of the Lord by beginning to do as must be done in his kingdom.

They could not rid themselves of their sins, but they could set about sending them away; they could quarrel with them, and proceed to turn them out of the house: the Lord was on his way to do his part in their final banishment. Those who had repented to the sending away of their sins, he would baptize with a holy power to send them away indeed. The operant will to get rid of them would be baptized with a fire that should burn them up. When a man breaks with his sins, then the wind of the Lord's fan will blow them away, the fire of the Lord's heart will consume them.

I think, then, that the part of the repentant man, and not the part of God, in the sending away of sins, is intended here. It is the man's one preparation for receiving the power to overcome them, the baptism of fire.

Not seldom, what comes in the name of the gospel of Jesus Christ, must seem, even to one not far from the kingdom of heaven, no good news at all. It does not draw him; it wakes in him not a single hope. He has no desire after what it offers him as redemption. The God it gives him news of, is not one to whom he would draw nearer. But when such a man comes to see that the very God must be his Life, the heart of his consciousness; when he perceives that, rousing himself to put from him what is evil, and do the duty that lies at his door, he may fearlessly claim the help of him who 'loved him into being,' then his will immediately sides with his conscience; he begins to try to *be*; and—first thing toward being—to rid himself of what is antagonistic to all being, namely *wrong*. Multitudes will not even approach the appalling task, the labour and pain of *being*. God is doing his part, is undergoing the mighty toil of an age-long creation, endowing men with power to be; but few as yet are those who take up their part, who respond to the call of God, who will to be, who put forth a divine effort after real existence. To the many, the spirit of the prophet cries, 'Turn ye, and change your way! The kingdom of heaven is near you. Let your king possess his own. Let God throne himself in you, that his liberty be your life, and you free men. That he may enter, clear the house for him. Send away the bad things out of it. Depart from evil, and do good. The duty that lieth at thy door, do it, be it great or small.'

For indeed in this region there is no great or small. 'Be content with your wages,' said the Baptist to the soldiers. To many people now, the word would be, 'Rule your temper;' or, 'Be courteous to all;' or, 'Let each hold the other better than himself;' or, 'Be just to your neighbour that you may love him.' To make straight in the desert a highway for our God, we must bestir ourselves in the very spot of the desert on which we stand; we must cast far from us our evil thing that blocks the way of his chariot-wheels. If we do not, never will those wheels roll through our streets; never will our desert blossom with his roses.

The message of John to his countrymen, was then, and is yet, the one message to the world:—'Send away your sins, for the kingdom of heaven is near.' Some of us—I cannot say *all*, for I do not know—who have already repented, who have long ago begun to send away our sins, need fresh repentance every day—how many times a day, God only knows. We are so ready to get upon some path that seems to run parallel with the narrow way, and then take no note of its divergence! What is there for us when we discover that we are out of the way, but to bethink ourselves and turn? By those 'who need no repentance,' the Lord may have meant such as had repented perfectly, had sent away all their sins, and were now with him in his Father's house; also such as have never sinned, and such as no longer turn aside for any temptation.

We shall now, perhaps, be able to understand the relation of the Lord himself to the baptism of John.

He came to John to be baptized; and most would say John's baptism was of repentance for the remission or pardon of sins. But the Lord could not be baptized for the remission of sins, for he had never done a selfish, an untrue, or an unfair thing. He had never wronged his Father, any more than ever his Father had wronged him. Happy, happy Son and Father, who had never either done the other wrong, in thought, word, or deed! As little had he wronged brother or sister. He needed no forgiveness; there was nothing to forgive. No more could he be baptized for repentance: in him repentance would have been to turn to evil! Where then was the propriety of his coming to be baptized by John, and insisting on being by him baptized? It must lie elsewhere.

If we take the words of John to mean 'the baptism of repentance unto the sending away of sins;' and if we bear in mind that in his case repentance could not be, inasmuch as what repentance is necessary to bring about in man, was already existent in Jesus; then, altering the words to fit the case, and saying, 'the baptism of willed devotion to the sending away of sin,' we shall see at once how the baptism of Jesus was a thing right and fit.

That he had no sin to repent of, was not because he was so constituted that he could not sin if he would; it was because, of his own will and judgment, he sent sin away from him—sent it from him with the full choice and energy of his nature. God knows good and evil, and, blessed be his name, chooses good. Never will his righteous anger make him unfair to us, make him forget that we are dust. Like him, his son also chose good, and in that choice resisted all temptation to help his fellows otherwise than as their and his father would. Instead of crushing the power of evil by divine force; instead of compelling justice and destroying the wicked; instead of making peace on the earth by the rule of a perfect prince; instead of gathering the children of Jerusalem under his wings whether they would or not, and saving them from the horrors that anguished his prophetic soul—he let evil work its will while it lived; he contented himself with the slow unencouraging ways of help essential; making men good; casting out, not merely controlling Satan; carrying to their perfect issue on earth the old primeval principles because of which the Father honoured him: 'Thou hast loved righteousness and hated iniquity; therefore God, even thy God, hath anointed thee with the oil of gladness above thy fellows.' To love righteousness is to make it grow, not to avenge it; and to win for righteousness the true victory, he, as well as his brethren, had to send away evil. Throughout his life on earth, he resisted every impulse to work more rapidly for a lower good,—strong perhaps when he saw old age and innocence and righteousness trodden under foot. What but this gives any worth of reality to the temptation in the wilderness, to the devil's departing from him for a season, to his coming again to experience a like failure? Ever and ever, in the whole attitude of his being, in his heart always lifted up, in his unfailing readiness to pull with the Father's yoke, he was repelling, driving away sin—away from himself, and, as Lord of men, and their saviour, away from others also, bringing them to abjure it like himself. No man, least of all any lord of men, can be good without willing to be good, without setting himself against evil, without sending away sin. Other men have to send it away out of them; the Lord had to send it away from before him, that it should not enter into him. Therefore is the stand against sin common to the captain of salvation and the soldiers under him.

What did Jesus come into the world to do? The will of God in saving his people from their sins—not from the punishment of their sins, that blessed aid to repentance, but from their sins themselves, the paltry as well as the heinous, the venial as well as the loathsome. His whole work was and is to send away sin—to banish it from the earth, yea, to cast it into the abyss of non-existence behind the back of God. His was the holy war; he came carrying it into our world; he resisted unto blood; the soldiers that followed him he taught and trained to resist also unto blood, striving against sin; so he became the captain of their salvation, and they, freed themselves, fought and suffered for others. This was the task to which he was baptized; this is yet his enduring labour. 'This is my blood of the new covenant which is shed for many unto the sending away of sins.' What was the new covenant? 'I will make a new covenant with the house of Israel and with the house of Judah; not according to the covenant which they brake, but this: I will put my law in their inward parts, and write it in their hearts, and will be their God, and they shall be my people.'

John baptized unto repentance because those to whom he was sent had to repent. They must bethink themselves, and send away the sin that was in them. But had there been a man, aware of no sin in him, but aware that life would be no life were not sin kept out of him, that man would have been right in receiving the baptism of John unto the continuous dismission of the sin ever wanting to enter in at his door. The object of the baptism was the sending away of sin; its object was repentance only where necessary to, only as introducing, as resulting in that. He to whom John was not sent, He whom he did not call, He who needed no repentance, was baptized for the same object, to the same conflict for the same end—the banishment of sin from the dominions of his father—and that first by his own sternest repudiation of it in himself. Thence came his victory in the wilderness: he would have his fathers way, not his own. Could he be less fitted to receive the baptism of John, that the object of it was no new thing with him, who had been about it from the beginning, yea, from all eternity? We shall be about it, I presume, to all eternity.

Such, then, as were baptized by John, were initiated into the company of those whose work was to send sin out of the world, and first, by sending it out of themselves, by having done with it. Their earliest endeavour in this direction would, as I have said, open the door for that help to enter without which a man could never succeed in the divinely arduous task—could not, because the region in which the work has to be wrought lies in the very roots of his own being, where, knowing nothing of the secrets of his essential existence, he can immediately do nothing, where the maker of him alone is potent, alone is consciously present. The change that must pass in him more than equals a new creation, inasmuch as it is a higher creation. But its necessity is involved in the former creation; and thence we have a right to ask help of our creator, for he requires of us what he has created us unable to effect without him. Nay, nay!—could we do anything without him, it were a thing to leave undone. Blessed fact that he hath made us so near him! that the scale of our being is so large, that we are completed only by his presence in it! that we are not men without him! that we can be one with our self-existent creator! that we are not cut off from the original Infinite! that in him we must share infinitude, or be enslaved by the finite! The very patent of our royalty is, that not for a moment can we live our true life without the eternal life present in and with our spirits. Without him at our unknown root, we cease to be. True, a dog cannot live without the presence of God; but I presume a dog may live a good dog-life without knowing the presence of his origin: man is dead if he know not the Power which is his cause, his deepest selfing self; the Presence which is not himself, and is nearer to him than himself; which is infinitely more himself, more his very being, than he is himself. The being of which we are conscious, is not our full self; the extent of our consciousness of our self is no measure of our self; our consciousness is infinitely less than we; while God is more necessary even to that poor consciousness of self than our self-consciousness is necessary to our humanity. Until a man become the power of his own existence, become his own God, the sole thing necessary to his existing is the will of God; for the well-being and perfecting of that existence, the sole thing necessary is, that the man should know his maker present in him. All that the children want is their Father.

The one true end of all speech concerning holy things is—the persuading of the individual man to cease to do evil, to set himself to do well, to look to the lord of his life to be on his side in the new struggle. Supposing the suggestions I have made correct, I do not care that my reader should understand them, except it be to turn against the evil in him, and begin to cast it out. If this be not the result, it is of no smallest consequence whether he agree with my interpretation or not. If he do thus repent, it is of equally little consequence; for, setting himself to do the truth, he is on the way to know all things. Real knowledge has begun to grow possible for him.

I am not sure what the Lord means in the words, 'Thus it becometh us to fulfil all righteousness.' Baptism could not be the fulfilling of all righteousness! Perhaps he means, 'We must, by a full act of the will, give ourselves altogether to righteousness. We must make it the business of our lives to send away sin, and do the will of the Father. That is my work as much as the work of any man who must repent ere he can begin. I will not be left out when you call men to be pure as our father is pure.'

To be certain whom he intends by *us* might perhaps help us to see his meaning. Does he intend *all of us men*? Does he intend 'my father and me'? Or does he intend 'you and me, John'? If the saying mean what I have suggested, then the *us* would apply to all that have the knowledge of good and evil. 'Every being that can, must devote himself to righteousness. To be right is no adjunct of completeness; it is the ground and foundation of existence.' But perhaps it was a lesson for John himself, who, mighty preacher of righteousness as he was, did not yet count it the all of life. I cannot tell.

Note that when the Lord began his teaching, he employed, neither using nor inculcating any rite, the same words as John,—'Repent, for the kingdom of heaven is at hand.'

That kingdom had been at hand all his infancy, boyhood, and young manhood: he was in the world with his father in his heart: that was the kingdom of heaven. Lonely man on the hillside, or boy the cynosure of doctor-eyes, his father was everything to him:—'Wist ye not that I must be in my father's things?'

*JESUS IN THE WORLD.*

'Son, why hast thou thus dealt with us? behold, thy father and I have sought thee sorrowing.' And he said unto them, 'How is it that ye sought me? wist ye not that I must be about my father's business?' And they understood not the saying which he spake unto them.—*Luke* ii. 48-50.

Was that his saying? Why did they not understand it? Do we understand it? What did his saying mean? The Greek is not absolutely clear. Whether the Syriac words he used were more precise, who in this world can tell? But had we heard his very words, we too, with his father and mother, would have failed to understand them. Must we fail still?

It will show at once where our initial difficulty lies, if I give the latter half of the saying as presented in the revised English version: its departure from the authorized reveals the point of obscurity:—'Wist ye not that I must be in my father's house?' His parents had his exact words, yet did not understand. We have not his exact words, and are in doubt as to what the Greek translation of them means.

If the authorized translation be true to the intent of the Greek, and therefore to that of the Syriac, how could his parents, knowing him as they did from all that had been spoken before concerning him, from all they had seen in him, from the ponderings in Mary's own heart, and from the precious thoughts she and Joseph cherished concerning him, have failed to understand him when he said that wherever he was, he must be about his father's business? On the other hand, supposing them to know and feel that he must be about his father's business, would that have been reason sufficient, in view of the degree of spiritual development to which they had attained, for the Lord's expecting them not to be anxious about him when they had lost him? Thousands on thousands who trust God for their friends in things spiritual, do not trust him for them in regard of their mere health or material well-being. His parents knew how prophets had always been treated in the land; or if they did not think in that direction, there were many dangers to which a boy like him would seem exposed, to rouse an anxiety that could be met only by a faith equal to saying, 'Whatever has happened to him, death itself, it can be no evil to one who is about his father's business;' and such a faith I think the Lord could not yet have expected of them. That what the world counts misfortune might befall him on his father's business, would have been recognized by him, I think, as reason for their parental anxiety—so long as they had not learned God—that he is what he is—the thing the Lord had come to teach his father's men and women. His words seem rather to imply that there was no need to be anxious about his personal safety. Fear of some accident to him seems to have been the cause of their trouble; and he did not mean, I think, that they ought not to mind if he died doing his father's will, but that he was in no danger as regarded accident or misfortune. This will appear more plainly as we proceed. So much for the authorized version.

Let us now take the translation given us by the Revisers:—'Wist ye not that I must be in my father's house?'

Are they authorized in translating the Greek thus? I know no justification for it, but am not learned enough to say they have none. That the Syriac has it so, is of little weight; seeing it is no original Syriac, but retranslation. If he did say *'my father's house'*, could he have meant the temple and his parents not have known what he meant? And why should he have taken it for granted they would know, or judge that they ought to have known, that he was there? So little did the temple suggest itself to them, that either it was the last place in which they sought him, or they had been there before, and had *not* found him. If he meant that they might have known this without being told, why was it that, even when he set the thing before them, they did not understand him? I do not believe he meant the temple; I do not think he said or meant *'in my fathers house'*.

What then makes those who give us this translation, prefer it to the phrase in the authorized version, *'about my Father's business'*?

One or other of two causes—most likely both together: an ecclesiastical fancy, and the mere fact that he was found in the temple. A mind ecclesiastical will presume the temple the fittest, therefore most likely place, for the Son of God to betake himself to, but such a mind would not be the first to reflect that the temple was a place where the Father was worshipped neither in spirit nor in truth—a place built by one of the vilest rulers of this world, less fit than many another spot for the special presence of him of whom the prophet bears witness: 'Thus saith the high and lofty One that inhabiteth eternity, whose name is Holy; I dwell in the high and holy place, with him also that is of a contrite and humble spirit, to revive the spirit of the humble, and to revive the heart of the contrite ones.' Jesus himself, with the same breath in which once he called it his father's house, called it a den of thieves. His expulsion from it of the buyers and sellers, was the first waft of the fan with which he was come to purge his father's dominions. Nothing could ever cleanse that house; his fanning rose to a tempest, and swept it out of his father's world.

For the second possible cause of the change from *business* to *temple*—the mere fact that he was found in the temple, can hardly be a reason for his expecting his parents to know that he was there; and if it witnessed to some way of thought or habit of his with which they were acquainted, it is, I repeat, difficult to see why the parents should fail to perceive what the interpreters have found so easily. But the parents looked for a larger meaning in the words of such a son—whose meaning at the same time was too large for them to find.

When, according to the Greek, the Lord, on the occasion already alluded to, says 'my father's house,' he says it plainly; he uses the word *house*: here he does not.

Let us see what lies in the Greek to guide us to the thought in the mind of the Lord when he thus reasoned with the apprehensions of his father and mother. The Greek, taken literally, says, 'Wist ye not that I must be in the——of my father?' The authorized version supplies *business*; the revised, *house*. There is no noun in the Greek, and the article 'the' is in the plural. To translate it as literally as it can be translated, making of it an English sentence, the saying stands, 'Wist ye not that I must be in the things of my father?' The plural article implies the English *things*; and the question is then, What *things* does he mean? The word might mean *affairs* or *business*; but why the plural article should be contracted to mean *house*, *I* do not know. In a great wide sense, no doubt, the word *house* might be used, as I am about to show, but surely not as meaning the temple.

He was arguing for confidence in God on the part of his parents, not for a knowledge of his whereabout. The same thing that made them anxious concerning him, prevented them from understanding his words—lack, namely, of faith in the Father. This, the one thing he came into the world to teach men, those words were meant to teach his parents. They are spirit and life, involving the one principle by which men shall live. They hold the same core as his words to his disciples in the storm, 'Oh ye of little faith!' Let us look more closely at them.

'Why did you look for me? Did you not know that I must be among my father's things?' What are we to understand by 'my father's things'? The translation given in the authorized version is, I think, as to the words themselves, a thoroughly justifiable one: 'I must be about my father's business,' or 'my father's affairs'; I refuse it for no other reason than that it does not fit the logic of the narrative, as does the word *things*, which besides opens to us a door of large and joyous prospect. Of course he was about his father's business, and they might know it and yet be anxious about him, not having a perfect faith in that father. But, as I have said already, it was not anxiety as to what might befall him because of doing the will of the Father; he might well seem to them as yet too young for danger from that source; it was but the vague perils of life beyond their sight that appalled them; theirs was just the uneasiness that possesses every parent whose child is missing; and if they, like him, had trusted in their father, they would have known what their son now meant when he said that he was in the midst of his father's things—namely, that the very things from which they dreaded evil accident, were his own home-surroundings; that he was not doing the Father's business in a foreign country, but in the Father's own house. Understood as meaning the world, or the universe, the phrase, 'my father's house,' would be a better translation than the authorized; understood as meaning the poor, miserable, God-forsaken temple—no more the house of God than a dead body is the house of a man—it is immeasurably inferior.

It seems to me, I say, that the Lord meant to remind them, or rather to make them feel, for they had not yet learned the fact, that he was never away from home, could not be lost, as they had thought him; that he was in his father's house all the time, where no hurt could come to him. 'The things' about him were the furniture and utensils of his home; he knew them all and how to use them. 'I must be among my father's belongings.' The world was his home because his father's house. He was not a stranger who did not know his way about in it. He was no lost child, but with his father all the time.

Here we find one main thing wherein the Lord differs from us: we are not at home in this great universe, our father's house. We ought to be, and one day we shall be, but we are not yet. This reveals Jesus more than man, by revealing him more man than we. We are not complete men, we are not anything near it, and are therefore out of harmony, more or less, with everything in the house of our birth and habitation. Always struggling to make our home in the world, we have not yet succeeded. We are not at home in it, because we are not at home with the lord of the house, the father of the family, not one with our elder brother who is his right hand. It is only the son, the daughter, that abideth ever in the house. When we are true children, if not the world, then the universe will be our home, felt and known as such, the house we are satisfied with, and would not change. Hence, until then, the hard struggle, the constant strife we hold with *Nature*—as we call the things of our father; a strife invaluable for our development, at the same time manifesting us not yet men enough to be lords of the house built for us to live in. We cannot govern or command in it as did the Lord, because we are not at one with his father, therefore neither in harmony with his things, nor rulers over them. Our best power in regard to them is but to find out wonderful facts concerning them and their relations, and turn these facts to our uses on systems of our own. For we discover what we seem to discover, by working inward from without, while he works outward from within; and we shall never understand the world, until we see it in the direction in which he works making it—-namely from within outward. This of course we cannot do until we are one with him. In the meantime, so much are both we and his things his, that we can err concerning them only as he has made it possible for us to err; we can wander only in the direction of the truth—if but to find that we can find nothing.

Think for a moment how Jesus was at home among the things of his father. It seems to me, I repeat, a spiritless explanation of his words—that the temple was the place where naturally he was at home. Does he make the least lamentation over the temple? It is Jerusalem he weeps over—the men of Jerusalem, the killers, the stoners. What was his place of prayer? Not the temple, but the mountain-top.

Where does he find symbols whereby to speak of what goes on in the mind and before the face of his father in heaven? Not in the temple; not in its rites; not on its altars; not in its holy of holies; he finds them in the world and its lovely-lowly facts; on the roadside, in the field, in the vineyard, in the garden, in the house; in the family, and the commonest of its affairs—the lighting of the lamp, the leavening of the meal, the neighbour's borrowing, the losing of the coin, the straying of the sheep. Even in the unlovely facts also of the world which he turns to holy use, such as the unjust judge, the false steward, the faithless labourers, he ignores the temple. See how he drives the devils from the souls and bodies of men, as we the wolves from our sheepfolds! how before him the diseases, scaly and spotted, hurry and flee! The world has for him no chamber of terror. He walks to the door of the sepulchre, the sealed cellar of his father's house, and calls forth its four days dead. He rebukes the mourners, he stays the funeral, and gives back the departed children to their parents' arms. The roughest of its servants do not make him wince; none of them are so arrogant as to disobey his word; he falls asleep in the midst of the storm that threatens to swallow his boat. Hear how, on that same occasion, he rebukes his disciples! The children to tremble at a gust of wind in the house! God's little ones afraid of a storm! Hear him tell the watery floor to be still, and no longer toss his brothers! see the watery floor obey him and grow still! See how the wandering creatures under it come at his call! See him leave his mountain-closet, and go walking over its heaving surface to the help of his men of little faith! See how the world's water turns to wine! how its bread grows more bread at his word! See how he goes from the house for a while, and returning with fresh power, takes what shape he pleases, walks through its closed doors, and goes up and down its invisible stairs!

All his life he was among his father's things, either in heaven or in the world—not then only when they found him in the temple at Jerusalem. He is still among his father's things, everywhere about in the world, everywhere throughout the wide universe. Whatever he laid aside to come to us, to whatever limitations, for our sake, he stooped his regal head, he dealt with the things about him in such lordly, childlike manner as made it clear they were not strange to him, but the things of his father. He claimed none of them as his own, would not have had one of them his except through his father. Only as his father's could he enjoy them;—only as coming forth from the Father, and full of the Father's thought and nature, had they to him any existence. That the things were his fathers, made them precious things to him. He had no care for having, as men count having. All his having was in the Father. I wonder if he ever put anything in his pocket: I doubt if he had one. Did he ever say, 'This is mine, not yours'? Did he not say, 'All things are mine, therefore they are yours'? Oh for his liberty among the things of the Father! Only by knowing them the things of our Father, can we escape enslaving ourselves to them. Through the false, the infernal idea of *having*, of *possessing* them, we make them our tyrants, make the relation between them and us an evil thing. The world was a blessed place to Jesus, because everything in it was his father's. What pain must it not have been to him, to see his brothers so vilely misuse the Father's house by grasping, each for himself, at the family things! If the knowledge that a spot in the landscape retains in it some pollution, suffices to disturb our pleasure in the whole, how must it not have been with him, how must it not be with him now, in regard to the disfigurements and defilements caused by the greed of men, by their haste to be rich, in his father's lovely house!

Whoever is able to understand Wordsworth, or Henry Vaughan, when either speaks of the glorious insights of his childhood, will be able to imagine a little how Jesus must, in his eternal childhood, regard the world.

Hear what Wordsworth says:—

> Our birth is but a sleep and a forgetting:
> The Soul that rises with us, our life's Star,
> Hath had elsewhere its setting,
>   And cometh from afar:
> Not in entire forgetfulness,
> And not in utter nakedness,
>  But trailing clouds of glory do we come
> From God, who is our home:
>   Heaven lies about us in our infancy!
>     Shades of the prison-house begin to close
> Upon the growing Boy,
>  But he beholds the light, and whence it flows,
> He sees it in his joy;
>  The Youth, who daily farther from the east
> Must travel, still is Nature's Priest,
> And by the vision splendid
> Is on his way attended;
> At length the Man perceives it die away,
> And fade into the light of common day.

Hear what Henry Vaughan says:—

> Happy those early dayes, when I
> Shin'd in my angell-infancy!
> Before I understood this place
> Appointed for my second race,
> Or taught my soul to fancy ought
> But a white, celestiall thought;
> When yet I had not walkt above
> A mile or two, from my first love,
> And looking back—at that short space—
> Could see a glimpse of His bright-face;
> When on some gilded cloud, or flowre
> My gazing soul would dwell an houre,
> And in those weaker glories spy
> Some shadows of eternity;
> Before I taught my tongue to wound
> My conscience with a sinfull sound,

>  Or had the black art to dispence
>  A sev'rall sinne to ev'ry sence,
>  But felt through all this fleshly dresse
>  Bright shootes of everlastingnesse.
>   O how I long to travell back,
>  And tread again that ancient track!
>  That I might once more reach that plaine,
>  Where first I left my glorious traine;
>  From whence th' inlightned spirit sees
>  That shady City of palme trees.

Whoever has thus gazed on flower or cloud; whoever can recall poorest memory of the trail of glory that hung about his childhood, must have some faint idea how his father's house and the things in it always looked, and must still look to the Lord. With him there is no fading into the light of common day. He has never lost his childhood, the very essence of childhood being nearness to the Father and the outgoing of his creative love; whence, with that insight of his eternal childhood of which the insight of the little ones here is a fainter repetition, he must see everything as the Father means it. The child sees things as the Father means him to see them, as he thought of them when he uttered them. For God is not only the father of the child, but of the childhood that constitutes him a child, therefore the childness is of the divine nature. The child may not indeed be capable of looking into the father's method, but he can in a measure understand his work, has therefore free entrance to his study and workshop both, and is welcome to find out what he can, with fullest liberty to ask him questions. There are men too, who, at their best, see, in their lower measure, things as they are—as God sees them always. Jesus saw things just as his father saw them in his creative imagination, when willing them out to the eyes of his children. But if he could always see the things of his father even as some men and more children see them at times, he might well feel *almost* at home among them. He could not cease to admire, cease to love them. I say *love*, because the life in them, the presence of the creative one, would ever be plain to him. In the Perfect, would familiarity ever destroy wonder at things essentially wonderful because essentially divine? To cease to wonder is to fall plumb-down from the childlike to the commonplace—the most undivine of all moods intellectual. Our nature can never be at home among things that are not wonderful to us.

Could we see things always as we have sometimes seen them—and as one day we must always see them, only far better—should we ever know dullness? Greatly as we might enjoy all forms of art, much as we might learn through the eyes and thoughts of other men, should we fly to these for deliverance from *ennui*, from any haunting discomfort? Should we not just open our own child-eyes, look upon the things themselves, and be consoled?

Jesus, then, would have his parents understand that he was in his father's world among his father's things, where was nothing to hurt him; he knew them all, was in the secret of them all, could use and order them as did his father. To this same I think all we humans are destined to rise. Though so many of us now are ignorant what kind of home we need, what a home we are capable of having, we too shall inherit the earth with the Son eternal, doing with it as we would—willing with the will of the Father. To such a home as we now inhabit, only perfected, and perfectly beheld, we are travelling—never to reach it save by the obedience that makes us the children, therefore the heirs of God. And, thank God! there the father does not die that the children may inherit; for, bliss of heaven! we inherit with the Father.

All the dangers of Jesus came from the priests, and the learned in the traditional law, whom his parents had not yet begun to fear on his behalf. They feared the dangers of the rugged way, the thieves and robbers of the hill-road. For the scribes and the pharisees, the priests and the rulers—they would be the first to acknowledge their Messiah, their king! Little they imagined, when they found him where he ought to have been safest had it been indeed his father's house, that there he sat amid lions—the great doctors of the temple! He could rule all the *things* in his father's house, but not the men of religion, the men of the temple, who called his father their Father. True, he might have compelled them with a word, withered them by a glance, with a finger-touch made them grovel at his feet; but such supremacy over his brothers the Lord of life despised. He must rule them as his father ruled himself; he would have them know themselves of the same family with himself; have them at home among the things of God, caring for the things he cared for, loving and hating as he and his father loved and hated, ruling themselves by the essential laws of being. Because they would not be such, he let them do to him as they would, that he might get at their hearts by some unknown unguarded door in their diviner part. 'I will be God among you; I will be myself to you.—You will not have me? Then do to me as you will. The created shall have power over him through whom they were created, that they may be compelled to know him and his father. They shall look on him whom they have pierced.'

His parents found him in the temple; they never really found him until he entered the true temple—their own adoring hearts. The temple that knows not its builder, is no temple; in it dwells no divinity. But at length he comes to his own, and his own receive him;—comes to them in the might of his mission to preach good tidings to the poor, to heal the broken-hearted, to preach deliverance, and sight, and liberty, and the Lord's own good time.

*JESUS AND HIS FELLOW TOWNSMEN.*

And he came to Nazareth, where he had been brought up: and, as his custom was, he went into the synagogue on the sabbath day, and stood up for to read. And there was delivered unto him the book of the prophet Esaias. And when he had opened the book, he found the place where it was written, 'The spirit of the Lord is upon me, because he hath anointed me to preach the gospel to the poor; he hath sent me to heal the brokenhearted, to preach deliverance to the captives, and recovering of sight to the blind, to set at liberty them that are bruised, to preach the acceptable year of the Lord.' And he closed the book, and he gave it again to the minister, and sat down. And the eyes of all them that were in the synagogue were fastened on him. And he began to say unto them, 'This day is this scripture fulfilled in your ears.'—*Luke* iv. 14-21.

The Lord's sermon upon the mount seems such an enlargement of these words of the prophet as might, but for the refusal of the men of Nazareth to listen to him, have followed his reading of them here recorded. That, as given by the evangelist, they correspond to neither of the differing originals of the English and Greek versions, ought to be enough in itself to do away with the spiritually vulgar notion of the verbal inspiration of the Scriptures.

The point at which the Lord stops in his reading, is suggestive: he closes the book, leaving the words 'and the day of vengeance of our God,' or, as in the Septuagint, 'the day of recompense,' unread: God's vengeance is as holy a thing as his love, yea, is love, for God is love and God is not vengeance; but, apparently, the Lord would not give the word a place in his announcement of his mission: his hearers would not recognize it as a form of the Father's love, but as vengeance on their enemies, not vengeance on the selfishness of those who would not be their brother's keeper.

He had not begun with Nazareth, neither with Galilee. 'A prophet has no honour in his own country,' he said, and began to teach where it was more likely he would be heard. It is true that he wrought his first miracle in Cana, but that was at his mother's request, not of his own intent, and he did not begin his teaching there. He went first to Jerusalem, there cast out the buyers and sellers from the temple, and did other notable things alluded to by St John; then went back to Galilee, where, having seen the things he did in Jerusalem, his former neighbours were now prepared to listen to him. Of these the Nazarenes, to whom the sight of him was more familiar, retained the most prejudice against him: he belonged to their very city! they had known him from a child!—and low indeed are they in whom familiarity with the high and true breeds contempt! they are judged already. Yet such was the fame of the new prophet, that even they were willing to hear in the synagogue what he had to say to them—thence to determine for themselves what claim he had to an honourable reception. But the eye of their judgment was not single, therefore was their body full of darkness. Should Nazareth indeed prove, to their self-glorifying satisfaction, the city of the great Prophet, they were more than ready to grasp at the renown of having produced him: he was indeed the great Prophet, and within a few minutes they would have slain him for the honour of Israel. In the ignoble even the love of their country partakes largely of the ignoble.

There was a shadow of the hateless vengeance of God in the expulsion of the dishonest dealers from the temple with which the Lord initiated his mission: that was his first parable to Jerusalem; to Nazareth he comes with the sweetest words of the prophet of hope in his mouth—good tidings of great joy—of healing and sight and liberty; followed by the godlike announcement, that what the prophet had promised he was come to fulfil. His heart, his eyes, his lips, his hands—his whole body is full of gifts for men, and that day was that scripture fulfilled in their ears. The prophecy had gone before that he should save his people from their sins; he brings an announcement they will better understand: he is come, he says, to deliver men from sorrow and pain, ignorance and oppression, everything that makes life hard and unfriendly. What a gracious speech, what a daring pledge to a world whelmed in tyranny and wrong! To the women of it, I imagine, it sounded the sweetest, in them woke the highest hopes. They had scarce had a hearing when the Lord came; and thereupon things began to mend with them, and are mending still, for the Lord is at work, and will be. He is the refuge of the oppressed. By its very woes, as by bitterest medicine, he is setting the world free from sin and woe. This very hour he is curing its disease, the symptoms of which are so varied and so painful; working none the less faithfully that the sick, taking the symptoms for the disease, cry out against the incompetence of their physician. 'What power can heal the broken-hearted?' they cry. And indeed it takes a God to do it, but the God is here! In yet better words than those of the prophet, spoken straight from his own heart, he cries: 'Come unto me, all ye that labour and are heavy laden, and I will give you rest.' He calls to him every heart knowing its own bitterness, speaks to the troubled consciousness of every child of the Father. He is come to free us from everything that makes life less than bliss essential. No other could be a gospel worthy of the God of men.

Every one will, I presume, confess to more or less misery. Its apparent source may be this or that; its real source is, to use a poor figure, a dislocation of the juncture between the created and the creating life. This primal evil is the parent of evils unnumbered, hence of miseries multitudinous, under the weight of which the arrogant man cries out against life, and goes on to misuse it, while the child looks around for help—and who shall help him but his father! The Father is with him all the time, but it may be long ere the child knows himself in his arms. His heart may be long troubled as well as his outer life. The dank mists of doubtful thought may close around his way, and hide from him the Light of the world! cold winds from the desert of foiled endeavour may sorely buffet and for a time baffle his hope; but every now and then the blue pledge of a great sky will break through the clouds over his head; and a faint aurora will walk his darkest East. Gradually he grows more capable of imagining a world in which every good thing thinkable may be a fact. Best of all, the story of him who is himself the good news, the gospel of God, becomes not only more and more believable to his heart, but more and more ministrant to his life of conflict, and his assurance of a living father who hears when his children cry. The gospel according to this or that expounder of it, may repel him unspeakably; the gospel according to Jesus Christ, attracts him supremely, and ever holds where it has drawn him. To the priest, the scribe, the elder, exclaiming against his self-sufficiency in refusing what they teach, he answers, 'It is life or death to me. Your gospel I cannot take. To believe as you would have me believe, would be to lose my God. Your God is no God to me. I do not desire him. I would rather die the death than believe in such a God. In the name of the true God, I cast your gospel from me; it is no gospel, and to believe it would be to wrong him in whom alone lies my hope.'

'But to believe in such a man,' he might go on to say, 'with such a message, as I read of in the New Testament, is life from the dead. I have yielded myself, to live no more in the idea of self, but with the life of God. To him I commit the creature he has made, that he may live in it, and work out its life—develop it according to the idea of it in his own creating mind. I fall in with his ways for me. I believe in him. I trust him. I try to obey him. I look to be rendered capable of and receive a pure vision of his will, freedom from the prison-house of my limitation, from the bondage of a finite existence. For the finite that dwells in the infinite and in which the infinite dwells, is finite no longer. Those who are thus children indeed, are little Gods, the divine brood of the infinite Father. No mere promise of deliverance from the consequences of sin, would be any gospel to me. Less than the liberty of a holy heart, less than the freedom of the Lord himself, will never satisfy one human soul. Father, set me free in the glory of thy will, so that I will only as thou willest. Thy will be at once thy perfection and mine. Thou alone art deliverance—absolute safety from every cause and kind of trouble that ever existed, anywhere now exists, or ever can exist in thy universe.'

But the people of the Lord's town, to whom he read, appropriating them, the gracious words of the prophet, were of the wise and prudent of their day. With one and the same breath, they seem to cry, 'These things are good, it is true, but they must come after our way. We must have the promise to our fathers fulfilled—that we shall rule the world, the chosen of God, the children of Abraham and Israel. We want to be a free people, manage our own affairs, live in plenty, and do as we please. Liberty alone can ever cure the woes of which you speak. We do not need to be better; we are well enough. Give us riches and honour, and keep us content with ourselves, that we may be satisfied with our own likeness, and thou shalt be the Messiah.' Never, perhaps, would such be men's spoken words, but the prevailing condition of their minds might often well take form in such speech. Whereon will they ground their complaint should God give them their hearts' desire? When that desire given closes in upon them with a torturing sense of slavery; when they find that what they have imagined their own will, was but a suggestion they knew not whence; when they discover that life is not good, yet they cannot die; will they not then turn and entreat their maker to save them after his own fashion?

Let us try to understand the brief, elliptical narrative of what took place in the synagogue of Nazareth on the occasion of our Lord's announcement of his mission.

'This day,' said Jesus, 'is this scripture fulfilled in your ears;' and went on with his divine talk. We shall yet know, I trust, what 'the gracious words' were 'which proceeded out of his mouth': surely some who heard them, still remember them, for 'all bare him witness, and wondered at' them! How did they bear him witness? Surely not alone by the intensity of their wondering gaze! Must not the narrator mean that their hearts bore witness to the power of his presence, that they felt the appeal of his soul to theirs, that they said in themselves, 'Never man spake like this man'? Must not the light of truth in his face, beheld of such even as knew not the truth, have lifted their souls up truthward? Was it not the something true, common to all hearts, that bore the wondering witness to the graciousness of his words? Had not those words found a way to the pure human, that is, the divine in the men? Was it not therefore that they were drawn to him—all but ready to accept him?—on their own terms, alas, not his! For a moment he seemed to them a true messenger, but truth in him was not truth to them: had he been what they took him for, he would have been no saviour. They were, however, though partly by mistake, well disposed toward him, and it was with a growing sense of being honoured by his relation to them, and the property they had in him, that they said, 'Is not this Joseph's son?'

But the Lord knew what was in their hearts; he knew the false notion with which they were almost ready to declare for him; he knew also the final proof to which they were in their wisdom and prudence about to subject him. He did not look likely to be a prophet, seeing he had grown up among them, and had never shown any credentials: they had a right to proof positive! They had heard of wonderful things he had done in other places: why had they not first of all been done in *their* sight? Who had a claim equal to theirs? who so capable as they to pronounce judgment on his mission whether false or true: had they not known him from childhood? His words were gracious, but words were nothing: he must *do* something—something wonderful! Without such conclusive, satisfying proof, Nazareth at least would never acknowledge him!

They were quite ready for the honour of having any true prophet, such as it seemed not impossible the son of Joseph might turn out to be, recognized as their townsman, one of their own people: if he were such, theirs was the credit of having produced him! Then indeed they were ready to bear witness to him, take his part, adopt his cause, and before the world stand up for him! As to his being the Messiah, that was merest absurdity: did they not all know his father, the carpenter? He might, however, be the prophet whom so many of the best in the nation were at the moment expecting! Let him do something wonderful!

They were not a gracious people, or a good. The Lord saw their thought, and it was far from being to his mind. He desired no such reception as they were at present equal to giving a prophet. His mighty works were not meant for such as they—to convince them of what they were incapable of understanding or welcoming! Those who would not believe without signs and wonders, could never believe worthily with any number of them, and none should be given them! His mighty works were to rouse the love, and strengthen the faith of the meek and lowly in heart, of such as were ready to come to the light, and show that they were of the light. He knew how poor the meaning the Nazarenes put on the words he had read; what low expectations they had of the Messiah when most they longed for his coming. They did not hear the prophet while he read the prophet! At sight of a few poor little wonders, nothing to him, to them sufficient to prove him such a Messiah as *they* looked for, they would burst into loud acclaim, and rush to their arms, eager, his officers and soldiers, to open the one triumphant campaign against the accursed Romans, and sweep them beyond the borders of their sacred country. Their Messiah would make of their nation the redeemed of the Lord, themselves the favourites of his court, and the tyrants of the world! Salvation from their sins was not in their hearts, not in their imaginations, not at all in their thoughts. They had heard him read his commission to heal the broken-hearted; they would rush to break hearts in his name. The Lord knew them, and their vain expectations. He would have no such followers—no followers on false conceptions—no followers whom wonders would delight but nowise better! The Nazarenes were not yet of the sort that needed but one change to be his people. He had come to give them help; until they accepted his, they could have none to give him.

The Lord never did mighty work in proof of his mission; to help a growing faith in himself and his father, he would do anything! He healed those whom healing would deeper heal—those in whom suffering had so far done its work, that its removal also would carry it on. To the Nazarenes he would not manifest his power; they were not in a condition to get good from such manifestation: it would but confirm their present arrogance and ambition. Wonderful works can only nourish a faith already existent; to him who believes without it, a miracle *may* be granted. It was the Israelite indeed, whom the Lord met with miracle: 'Because I said unto thee, I saw thee under the fig-tree, believest thou? Thou shalt see the angels of God ascending and descending on the Son of Man.' Those who laughed him to scorn were not allowed to look on the resurrection of the daughter of Jairus. Peter, when he would walk on the water, had both permission and power given him to do so. The widow received the prophet, and was fed; the Syrian went to the prophet, and was cured. In Nazareth, because of unbelief, the Lord could only lay his hands on a few sick folk; in the rest was none of that leaning toward the truth, which alone can make room for the help of a miracle. This they soon made manifest.

The Lord saw them on the point of challenging a display of his power, and anticipated the challenge with a refusal.

For the better understanding of his words, let me presume to paraphrase them: 'I know you will apply to me the proverb, Physician, heal thyself, requiring me to prove what is said of me in Capernaum, by doing the same here; but there is another proverb, No prophet is accepted in his own country. Unaccepted I do nothing wonderful. In the great famine, Elijah was sent to no widow of the many in Israel, but to a Sidonian; and Elisha cured no leper of the many in Israel, but Naaman the Syrian. There are those fit to see signs and wonders; they are not always the kin of the prophet.'

The Nazarenes heard with indignation. Their wonder at his gracious words was changed to bitterest wrath. The very beams of their ugly religion were party-spirit, exclusiveness, and pride in the fancied favour of God for them only of all the nations: to hint at the possibility of a revelation of the glory of God to a stranger; far more, to hint that a stranger might be fitter to receive such a revelation than a Jew, was an offence reaching to the worst insult; and it was cast in their teeth by a common man of their own city! 'Thou art but a well-known carpenter's son, and dost thou teach *us*! Darest thou imply a divine preference for Capernaum over Nazareth?' In bad odour with the rest of their countrymen, they were the prouder of themselves.

The *whole* synagogue, observe, rose in a fury. Such a fellow a prophet! He was worse than the worst of Gentiles! he was a false Jew! a traitor to his God! a friend of the idol-worshipping Romans! Away with him! His townsmen led the van in his rejection by his own. The men of Nazareth would have forestalled his crucifixion by them of Jerusalem. What! a Sidonian woman fitter to receive the prophet than any Jewess! a heathen worthier to be kept alive by miracle in time of famine, than a worshipper of the true God! a leper of Damascus less displeasing to God than the lepers of his chosen race! It was no longer condescending approval that shone in their eyes. He a prophet! They had seen through him! Soon had they found him out! The moment he perceived it useless to pose for a prophet with them, who had all along known the breed of him, he had turned to insult them! He dared not attempt in his own city the deceptions with which, by the help of Satan, he had made such a grand show, and fooled the idiots of Capernaum! He saw they knew him too well, were too wide-awake to be cozened by him, and to avoid their expected challenge, fell to reviling the holy nation. Let him take the consequences! To the brow of the hill with him!

How could there be any miracle for such! They were well satisfied with themselves, and

> Nothing almost sees miracles
> But misery.

Need and the upward look, the mood ready to believe when and where it can, the embryonic faith, is dear to Him whose love would have us trust him. Let any man seek him—not in curious inquiry whether the story of him may be true or cannot be true—in humble readiness to accept him altogether if only he can, and he shall find him; we shall not fail of help to believe because we doubt. But if the questioner be such that the dispersion of his doubt would but leave him in disobedience, the Power of truth has no care to effect his conviction. Why cast out a devil that the man may the better do the work of the devil? The childlike doubt will, as it softens and yields, minister nourishment with all that was good in it to the faith-germ at its heart; the wise and prudent unbelief will be left to develop its own misery. The Lord could easily have satisfied the Nazarenes that he was the Messiah: they would but have hardened into the nucleus of an army for the subjugation of the world. To a warfare with their own sins, to the subjugation of their doing and desiring to the will of the great Father, all the miracles in his power would never have persuaded them. A true convincement is not possible to hearts and minds like theirs. Not only is it impossible for a low man to believe a thousandth part of what a noble man can, but a low man cannot believe anything as a noble man believes it. The men of Nazareth could have believed in Jesus as their saviour from the Romans; as their saviour from their sins they could not believe in him, for they loved their sins. The king of heaven came to offer them a share in his kingdom; but they were not poor in spirit, and the kingdom of heaven was not for them. Gladly would they have inherited the earth; but they were not meek, and the earth was for the lowly children of the perfect Father.

*THE HEIRS OF HEAVEN AND EARTH.*

And he opened his mouth and taught them, saying, 'Blessed are the poor in spirit; for theirs is the kingdom of heaven.' ...'Blessed are the meek; for they shall inherit the earth.'—*Matthew* v. 2, 3, 5.

The words of the Lord are the seed sown by the sower. Into our hearts they must fall that they may grow. Meditation and prayer must water them, and obedience keep them in the sunlight. Thus will they bear fruit for the Lord's gathering.

Those of his disciples, that is, obedient hearers, who had any experience in trying to live, would, in part, at once understand them; but as they obeyed and pondered, the meaning of them would keep growing. This we see in the writings of the apostles. It will be so with us also, who need to understand everything he said neither more nor less than they to whom first he spoke; while our obligation to understand is far greater than theirs at the time, inasmuch as we have had nearly two thousand years' experience of the continued coming of the kingdom he then preached: it is not yet come; it has been all the time, and is now, drawing slowly nearer.

The sermon on the mount, as it is commonly called, seems the Lord's first free utterance, in the presence of any large assembly, of the good news of the kingdom. He had been teaching his disciples and messengers; and had already brought the glad tidings that his father was their father, to many besides—to Nathanael for one, to Nicodemus, to the woman of Samaria, to every one he had cured, every one whose cry for help he had heard: his epiphany was a gradual thing, beginning, where it continues, with the individual. It is impossible even to guess at what number may have heard him on this occasion: he seems to have gone up the mount because of the crowd—to secure a somewhat opener position whence he could better speak; and thither followed him those who desired to be taught of him, accompanied doubtless by not a few in whom curiosity was the chief motive. Disciple or gazer, he addressed the individuality of every one that had ears to hear. Peter and Andrew, James and John, are all we know as his recognized disciples, followers, and companions, at the time; but, while his words were addressed to such as had come to him desiring to learn of him, the things he uttered were eternal truths, life in which was essential for every one of his father's children, therefore they were for all: he who heard to obey, was his disciple.

How different, at the first sound of it, must the good news have been from the news anxiously expected by those who waited for the Messiah! Even the Baptist in prison lay listening after something of quite another sort. The Lord had to send him a message, by eye-witnesses of his doings, to remind him that God's thoughts are not as our thoughts, or his ways as our ways—that the design of God is other and better than the expectation of men. His summary of the gifts he was giving to men, culminated with the preaching of the good news to the poor. If John had known these his doings before, he had not recognized them as belonging to the Lord's special mission: the Lord tells him it is not enough to have accepted him as the Messiah; he must recognize his doings as the work he had come into the world to do, and as in their nature so divine as to be the very business of the Son of God in whom the Father was well pleased.

Wherein then consisted the goodness of the news which he opened his mouth to give them? What was in the news to make the poor glad? Why was his arrival with such words in his heart and mouth, the coming of the kingdom?

All good news from heaven, is of *truth*—essential truth, involving duty, and giving and promising help to the performance of it. There can be no good news for us men, except of uplifting love, and no one can be lifted up who will not rise. If God himself sought to raise his little ones without their consenting effort, they would drop from his foiled endeavour. He will carry us in his arms till we are able to walk; he will carry us in his arms when we are weary with walking; he will not carry us if we will not walk.

Very different are the good news Jesus brings us from certain prevalent representations of the gospel, founded on the pagan notion that suffering is an offset for sin, and culminating in the vile assertion that the suffering of an innocent man, just because he is innocent, yea perfect, is a satisfaction to the holy Father for the evil deeds of his children. As a theory concerning the atonement nothing could be worse, either intellectually, morally, or spiritually; announced as the gospel itself, as the good news of the kingdom of heaven, the idea is monstrous as any Chinese dragon. Such a so-called gospel is no gospel, however accepted as God sent by good men of a certain development. It is evil news, dwarfing, enslaving, maddening—news to the child-heart of the dreariest damnation. Doubtless some elements of the gospel are mixed up with it on most occasions of its announcement; none the more is it the message received from him. It can be good news only to such as are prudently willing to be delivered from a God they fear, but unable to accept the gospel of a perfect God, in whom to trust perfectly.

The good news of Jesus was just the news of the thoughts and ways of the Father in the midst of his family. He told them that the way men thought for themselves and their children was not the way God thought for himself and his children; that the kingdom of heaven was founded, and must at length show itself founded on very different principles from those of the kingdoms and families of the world, meaning by the world that part of the Father's family which will not be ordered by him, will not even try to obey him. The world's man, its great, its successful, its honorable man, is he who may have and do what he pleases, whose strength lies in money and the praise of men; the greatest in the kingdom of heaven is the man who is humblest and serves his fellows the most. Multitudes of men, in no degree notable as ambitious or proud, hold the ambitious, the proud man in honour, and, for all deliverance, hope after some shadow of his prosperity. How many even of those who look for the world to come, seek to the powers of this world for deliverance from its evils, as if God were the God of the world to come only! The oppressed of the Lord's time looked for a Messiah to set their nation free, and make it rich and strong; the oppressed of our time believe in money, knowledge, and the will of a people which needs but power to be in its turn the oppressor. The first words of the Lord on this occasion were:—'Blessed are the poor in spirit, for theirs is the kingdom of heaven,'

It is not the proud, it is not the greedy of distinction, it is not those who gather and hoard, not those who lay down the law to their neighbours, not those that condescend, any more than those that shrug the shoulder and shoot out the lip, that have any share in the kingdom of the Father. That kingdom has no relation with or resemblance to the kingdoms of this world, deals with no one thing that distinguishes their rulers, except to repudiate it. The Son of God will favour no smallest ambition, be it in the heart of him who leans on his bosom. The kingdom of God, the refuge of the oppressed, the golden age of the new world, the real Utopia, the newest yet oldest Atlantis, the home of the children, will not open its gates to the most miserable who would rise above his equal in misery, who looks down on any one more miserable than himself. It is the home of perfect brotherhood. The poor, the beggars in spirit, the humble men of heart, the unambitious, the unselfish; those who never despise men, and never seek their praises; the lowly, who see nothing to admire in themselves, therefore cannot seek to be admired of others; the men who give themselves away—these are the freemen of the kingdom, these are the citizens of the new Jerusalem. The men who are aware of their own essential poverty; not the men who are poor in friends, poor in influence, poor in acquirements, poor in money, but those who are poor in spirit, who *feel themselves poor creatures*; who know nothing to be pleased with themselves for, and desire nothing to make them think well of themselves; who know that they need much to make their life worth living, to make their existence a good thing, to make them fit to live; these humble ones are the poor whom the Lord calls blessed. When a man says, I am low and worthless, then the gate of the kingdom begins to open to him, for there enter the true, and this man has begun to know the truth concerning himself. Whatever such a man has attained to, he straightway forgets; it is part of him and behind him; his business is with what he has not, with the things that lie above and before him. The man who is proud of anything he thinks he has reached, has not reached it. He is but proud of himself, and imagining a cause for his pride. If he had reached, he would already have begun to forget. He who delights in contemplating whereto he has attained, is not merely sliding back; he is already in the dirt of self-satisfaction. The gate of the kingdom is closed, and he outside. The child who, clinging to his Father, dares not think he has in any sense attained while as yet he is not as his Father—his Father's heart, his Father's heaven is his natural home. To find himself thinking of himself as above his fellows, would be to that child a shuddering terror; his universe would contract around him, his ideal wither on its throne. The least motion of self-satisfaction, the first thought of placing himself in the forefront of estimation, would be to him a flash from the nether abyss. God is his life and his lord. That his father should be content with him must be all his care. Among his relations with his neighbour, infinitely precious, comparison with his neighbour has no place. Which is the greater is of no account. He would not choose to be less than his neighbour; he would choose his neighbour to be greater than he. He looks up to every man. Otherwise gifted than he, his neighbour is more than he. All come from the one mighty father: shall he judge the live thoughts of God, which is greater and which is less? In thus denying, thus turning his back on himself, he has no thought of saintliness, no thought but of his father and his brethren. To such a child heaven's best secrets are open. He clambers about the throne of the Father unrebuked; his back is ready for the smallest heavenly playmate; his arms are an open refuge for any blackest little lost kid of the Father's flock; he will toil with it up the heavenly stair, up the very steps of the great white throne, to lay it on the Father's knees. For the glory of that Father is not in knowing himself God, but in giving himself away—in creating and redeeming and glorifying his children.

The man who does not house self, has room to be his real self—God's eternal idea of him. He lives eternally; in virtue of the creative power present in him with momently, unimpeded creation, he *is*. How should there be in him one thought of ruling or commanding or surpassing! He can imagine no bliss, no good in being greater than some one else. He is unable to wish himself other than he is, except more what God made him for, which is indeed the highest willing of the will of God. His brother's wellbeing is essential to his bliss. The thought of standing higher in the favour of God than his brother, would make him miserable. He would lift every brother to the embrace of the Father. Blessed are the poor in spirit, for they are of the same spirit as God, and of nature the kingdom of heaven is theirs.

'Blessed are the meek, for they shall inherit the earth,' expresses the same principle: the same law holds in the earth as in the kingdom of heaven. How should it be otherwise? Has the creator of the ends of the earth ceased to rule it after his fashion, because his rebellious children have so long, to their own hurt, vainly endeavoured to rule it after theirs? The kingdom of heaven belongs to the poor; the meek shall inherit the earth. The earth as God sees it, as those to whom the kingdom of heaven belongs also see it, is good, all good, very good, fit for the meek to inherit; and one day they shall inherit it—not indeed as men of the world count inheritance, but as the maker and owner of the world has from the first counted it. So different are the two ways of inheriting, that one of the meek may be heartily enjoying his possession, while one of the proud is selfishly walling him out from the spot in it he loves best.

The meek are those that do not assert themselves, do not defend themselves, never dream of avenging themselves, or of returning aught but good for evil. They do not imagine it their business to take care of themselves. The meek man may indeed take much thought, but it will not be for himself. He never builds an exclusive wall, shuts any honest neighbour out. He will not always serve the wish, but always the good of his neighbour. His service must be true service. Self shall be no umpire in affair of his. Man's consciousness of himself is but a shadow: the meek man's self always vanishes in the light of a real presence. His nature lies open to the Father of men, and to every good impulse is as it were empty. No bristling importance, no vain attendance of fancied rights and wrongs, guards his door, or crowds the passages of his house; they are for the angels to come and go. Abandoned thus to the truth, as the sparks from the gleaming river dip into the flowers of Dante's unperfected vision, so the many souls of the visible world, lights from the father of lights, enter his heart freely; and by them he inherits the earth he was created to inherit—possesses it as his father made him capable of possessing, and the earth of being possessed. Because the man is meek, his eye is single; he sees things as God sees them, as he would have his child see them: to confront creation with pure eyes is to possess it.

How little is the man able to make his own, who would ravish all! The man who, by the exclusion of others from the space he calls his, would grasp any portion of the earth as his own, befools himself in the attempt. The very bread he has swallowed cannot so in any real sense be his. There does not exist such a power of possessing as he would arrogate. There is not such a sense of having as that of which he has conceived the shadow in his degenerate and lapsing imagination. The real owner of his demesne is that pedlar passing his gate, into a divine soul receiving the sweetnesses which not all the greed of the so-counted possessor can keep within his walls: they overflow the cup-lip of the coping, to give themselves to the footfarer. The motions aerial, the sounds, the odours of those imprisoned spaces, are the earnest of a possession for which is ever growing his power of possessing. In no wise will such inheritance interfere with the claim of the man who calls them his. Each possessor has them his, as much as each in his own way is capable of possessing them. For possession is determined by the kind and the scope of the power of possessing; and the earth has a fourth dimension of which the mere owner of its soil knows nothing.

The child of the maker is naturally the inheritor. But if the child try to possess as a house the thing his father made an organ, will he succeed in so possessing it? Or if he do nestle in a corner of its case, will he oust thereby the Lord of its multiplex harmony, sitting regnant on the seat of sway, and drawing with 'volant touch' from the house of the child the liege homage of its rendered wealth? To the poverty of such a child are all those left, who think to have and to hold after the corrupt fancies of a greedy self.

We cannot see the world as God means it, save in proportion as our souls are meek. In meekness only are we its inheritors. Meekness alone makes the spiritual retina pure to receive God's things as they are, mingling with them neither imperfection nor impurity of its own. A thing so beheld that it conveys to me the divine thought issuing in its form, is mine; by nothing but its mediation between God and my life, can anything be mine. The man so dull as to insist that a thing is his because he has bought it and paid for it, had better bethink himself that not all the combined forces of law, justice, and goodwill, can keep it his; while even death cannot take the world from the man who possesses it as alone the maker of him and it cares that he should possess it. This man leaves it, but carries it with him; that man carries with him only its loss. He passes, unable to close hand or mouth upon any portion of it. Its *ownness* to him was but the changes he could make in it, and the nearness into which he could bring it to the body he lived in. That body the earth in its turn possesses now, and it lies very still, changing nothing, but being changed. Is this the fine of the great buyer of land, to have his fine pate full of fine dirt? In the soul of the meek, the earth remains an endless possession—his because he who made it is his—his as nothing but his maker could ever be the creature's. He has the earth by his divine relation to him who sent it forth from him as a tree sends out its leaves. To inherit the earth is to grow ever more alive to the presence, in it and in all its parts, of him who is the life of men. How far one may advance in such inheritance while yet in the body, will simply depend on the meekness he attains while yet in the body; but it may be, as Frederick Denison Maurice, the servant of God, thought while yet he was with us, that the new heavens and the new earth are the same in which we now live, righteously inhabited by the meek, with their deeper-opened eyes. What if the meek of the dead be thus possessing it even now! But I do not care to speculate. It is enough that the man who refuses to assert himself, seeking no recognition by men, leaving the care of his life to the Father, and occupying himself with the will of the Father, shall find himself, by and by, at home in the Father's house, with all the Father's property his.

Which is more the possessor of the world—he who has a thousand houses, or he who, without one house to call his own, has ten in which his knock at the door would rouse instant jubilation? Which is the richer—the man who, his large money spent, would have no refuge; or he for whose necessity a hundred would sacrifice comfort? Which of the two possessed the earth—king Agrippa or tent-maker Paul?

Which is the real possessor of a book—the man who has its original and every following edition, and shows, to many an admiring and envying visitor, now this, now that, in binding characteristic, with possessor-pride; yea, from secret shrine is able to draw forth and display the author's manuscript, with the very shapes in which his thoughts came forth to the light of day,—or the man who cherishes one little, hollow-backed, coverless, untitled, bethumbed copy, which he takes with him in his solitary walks and broods over in his silent chamber, always finding in it some beauty or excellence or aid he had not found before—which is to him in truth as a live companion?

For what makes the thing a book? Is it not that it has a soul—the mind in it of him who wrote the book? Therefore only can the book be possessed, for life alone can be the possession of life. The dead possess their dead only to bury them.

Does not he then, who loves and understands his book, possess it with such possession as is impossible to the other? Just so may the world itself be possessed—either as a volume unread, or as the wine of a soul, 'the precious life-blood of a master-spirit, embalmed and treasured up on purpose to a life beyond life.' It may be possessed as a book filled with words from the mouth of God, or but as the golden-clasped covers of that book; as an embodiment or incarnation of God himself; or but as a house built to sell. The Lord loved the world and the things of the world, not as the men of the world love them, but finding his father in everything that came from his father's heart.

The same spirit, then, is required for possessing the kingdom of heaven, and for inheriting the earth. How should it not be so, when the one Power is the informing life of both? If we are the Lord's, we possess the kingdom of heaven, and so inherit the earth. How many who call themselves by his name, would have it otherwise: they would possess the earth and inherit the kingdom! Such fill churches and chapels on Sundays: anywhere suits for the worship of Mammon.

Yet verily, earth as well as heaven may be largely possessed even now.

Two men are walking abroad together; to the one, the world yields thought after thought of delight; he sees heaven and earth embrace one another; he feels an indescribable presence over and in them; his joy will afterward, in the solitude of his chamber, break forth in song;—to the other, oppressed with the thought of his poverty, or ruminating how to make much into more, the glory of the Lord is but a warm summer day; it enters in at no window of his soul; it offers him no gift; for, in the very temple of God, he looks for no God in it. Nor must there needs be two men to think and feel thus differently. In what diverse fashion will any one *subject* to ever-changing mood see the same world of the same glad creator! Alas for men, if it changed as we change, if it grew meaningless when we grow faithless! Thought for a morrow that may never come, dread of the dividing death which works for endless companionship, anger with one we love, will cloud the radiant morning, and make the day dark with night. At evening, having bethought ourselves, and returned to him that feeds the ravens, and watches the dying sparrow, and says to his children 'Love one another,' the sunset splendour is glad over us, the western sky is refulgent as the court of the Father when the glad news is spread abroad that a sinner has repented. We have mourned in the twilight of our little faith, but, having sent away our sin, the glory of God's heaven over his darkening earth has comforted us.

*SORROW THE PLEDGE OF JOY.*

'Blessed are they that mourn, for they shall be comforted.'—*Matthew* v. 4.

Grief, then, sorrow, pain of heart, mourning, is no partition-wall between man and God. So far is it from opposing any obstacle to the passage of God's light into man's soul, that the Lord congratulates them that mourn. There is no evil in sorrow. True, it is not an essential good, a good in itself, like love; but it will mingle with any good thing, and is even so allied to good that it will open the door of the heart for any good. More of sorrowful than of joyful men are always standing about the everlasting doors that open into the presence of the Most High. It is true also that joy is in its nature more divine than sorrow; for, although man must sorrow, and God share in his sorrow, yet in himself God is not sorrowful, and the 'glad creator' never made man for sorrow: it is but a stormy strait through which he must pass to his ocean of peace. He 'makes the joy the last in every song.' Still, I repeat, a man in sorrow is in general far nearer God than a man in joy. Gladness may make a man forget his thanksgiving; misery drives him to his prayers. For we *are* not yet, we are only *becoming*. The endless day will at length dawn whose every throbbing moment will heave our hearts Godward; we shall scarce need to lift them up: now, there are two door-keepers to the house of prayer, and Sorrow is more on the alert to open than her grandson Joy.

The gladsome child runs farther afield; the wounded child turns to go home. The weeper sits down close to the gate; the lord of life draws nigh to him from within. God loves not sorrow, yet rejoices to see a man sorrowful, for in his sorrow man leaves his heavenward door on the latch, and God can enter to help him. He loves, I say, to see him sorrowful, for then he can come near to part him from that which makes his sorrow a welcome sight. When Ephraim bemoans himself, he is a pleasant child. So good a medicine is sorrow, so powerful to slay the moths that infest and devour the human heart, that the Lord is glad to see a man weep. He congratulates him on his sadness. Grief is an ill-favoured thing, but she is Love's own child, and her mother loves her.

The promise to them that mourn, is not *the kingdom of heaven*, but that their mourning shall be ended, that they shall be comforted. <u>To mourn is not to fight with evil; it is only to miss that which is good.</u> It is not an essential heavenly condition, like poorness of spirit or meekness. No man will carry his mourning with him into heaven—or, if he does, <u>it will speedily be turned either into joy, or into what will result in joy, namely, redemptive action.</u>

Mourning is a canker-bitten blossom on the rose-tree of love. Is there any mourning worthy the name that has not love for its root? Men mourn because they love. Love is the life out of which are fashioned all the natural feelings, every emotion of man. Love modelled by faith, is hope; love shaped by wrong, is anger—verily anger, though pure of sin; love invaded by loss, is grief.

The garment of mourning is oftenest a winding-sheet; the loss of the loved by death is the main cause of the mourning of the world. The Greek word here used to describe the blessed of the Lord, generally means *those that mourn for the dead*. It is not in the New Testament employed exclusively in this sense, neither do I imagine it stands here for such only: there are griefs than death sorer far, and harder far to comfort—harder even for God himself, with whom all things are possible; but it may give pleasure to know that the promise of comfort to those that mourn, may specially apply to those that mourn because their loved have gone out of their sight, and beyond the reach of their cry. Their sorrow, indeed, to the love divine, involves no difficulty; it is a small matter, easily met. The father, whose elder son is ever with him, but whose younger is in a far country, wasting his substance with riotous living, is unspeakably more to be pitied, and is harder to help, than that father both of whose sons lie in the sleep of death.

Much of what goes by the name of comfort, is merely worthless; and such as could be comforted by it, I should not care to comfort. Let time do what it may to bring the ease of oblivion; let change of scene do what in it lies to lead thought away from the vanished; let new loves bury grief in the grave of the old love: consolation of such sort could never have crossed the mind of Jesus. Would The Truth call a man blessed because his pain would sooner or later depart, leaving him at best no better than before, and certainly poorer—not only the beloved gone, but the sorrow for him too, and with the sorrow the love that had caused the sorrow? Blessed of God because restored to an absence of sorrow? Such a God were fitly adored only where not one heart worshipped in spirit and in truth.

'The Lord means of course,' some one may say, 'that the comfort of the mourners will be the restoration of that which they have lost. He means, "Blessed are ye although ye mourn, for your sorrow will be turned into joy."'

Happy are they whom nothing less than such restoration will comfort! But would such restoration be comfort enough for the heart of Jesus to give? Was ever love so deep, so pure, so perfect, as to be good enough for him? And suppose the love between the parted two had been such, would the mere restoration in the future of that which once he had, be ground enough for so emphatically proclaiming the man blessed now, blessed while yet in the midnight of his loss, and knowing nothing of the hour of his deliverance? To call a man *blessed* in his sorrow because of something to be given him, surely implies a something better than what he had before! True, the joy that is past may have been so great that the man might well feel blessed in the merest hope of its restoration; but would that be meaning enough for the word in the mouth of the Lord? That the interruption of his blessedness was but temporary, would hardly be fit ground for calling the man *blessed* in that interruption. *Blessed* is a strong word, and in the mouth of Jesus means all it can mean. Can his saying here mean less than—'Blessed are they that mourn, for they shall be comforted with a bliss well worth all the pain of the medicinal sorrow'? Besides, the benediction surely means that the man is blessed *because* of his condition of mourning, not in spite of it. His mourning is surely a part at least of the Lord's ground for congratulating him: is it not the present operative means whereby the consolation is growing possible? In a word, I do not think the Lord would be content to call a man blessed on the mere ground of his going to be restored to a former bliss by no means perfect; I think he congratulated the mourners upon the grief they were enduring, because he saw the excellent glory of the comfort that was drawing nigh; because he knew the immeasurably greater joy to which the sorrow was at once clearing the way and conducting the mourner. When I say *greater*, God forbid I should mean *other!* I mean the same bliss, divinely enlarged and divinely purified—passed again through the hands of the creative Perfection. The Lord knew all the history of love and loss; beheld throughout the universe the winged Love discrowning the skeleton Fear. God's comfort must ever be larger than man's grief, else were there gaps in his Godhood. Mere restoration would leave a hiatus, barren and growthless, in the development of his children.

But, alas, what a pinched hope, what miserable expectations, most who call themselves the Lord's disciples derive from their notions of his teaching! Well may they think of death as the one thing to be right zealously avoided, and for ever lamented! Who would forsake even the window-less hut of his sorrow for the poor mean place they imagine the Father's house! Why, many of them do not even expect to know their friends there! do not expect to distinguish one from another of all the holy assembly! They will look in many faces, but never to recognize old friends and lovers! A fine saviour of men is their Jesus! Glorious lights they shine in the world of our sorrow, holding forth a word of darkness, of dismallest death! Is the Lord such as they believe him? 'Good-bye, then, good Master!' cries the human heart. 'I thought thou couldst save me, but, alas, thou canst not. If thou savest the part of our being which can sin, thou lettest the part that can love sink into hopeless perdition: thou art not he that should come; I look for another! Thou wouldst destroy and not save me! Thy father is not my father; thy God is not my God! Ah, to whom shall we go? He has not the words of eternal life, this Jesus, and the universe is dark as chaos! O father, this thy son is good, but we need a greater son than he. Never will thy children love thee under the shadow of this new law, that they are not to love one another as thou lovest them!' How does that man love God—of what kind is the love he bears him—who is unable to believe that God loves every throb of every human heart toward another? Did not the Lord die that we should love one another, and be one with him and the Father, and is not the knowledge of difference essential to the deepest love? Can there be oneness without difference? harmony without distinction? Are all to have the same face? then why faces at all? If the plains of heaven are to be crowded with the same one face over and over for ever, but one moment will pass ere by monotony bliss shall have grown ghastly. Why not perfect spheres of featureless ivory rather than those multitudinous heads with one face! Or are we to start afresh with countenances all new, each beautiful, each lovable, each a revelation of the infinite father, each distinct from every other, and therefore all blending toward a full revealing—but never more the dear old precious faces, with its whole story in each, which seem, at the very thought of them, to draw our hearts out of our bosoms? Were they created only to become dear, and be destroyed? Is it in wine only that the old is better? Would such a new heaven be a thing to thank God for? Would this be a prospect on which the Son of Man would congratulate the mourner, or at which the mourner for the dead would count himself blessed? It is a shame that such a preposterous, monstrous unbelief should call for argument.

A heaven without human love it were inhuman, and yet more undivine to desire; it ought not to be desired by any being made in the image of God. The lord of life died that his father's children might grow perfect in love—might love their brothers and sisters as he loved them: is it to this end that they must cease to know one another? To annihilate the past of our earthly embodiment, would be to crush under the heel of an iron fate the very idea of tenderness, human or divine.

We shall all doubtless be changed, but in what direction?—to something less, or to something greater?—to something that is less we, which means degradation? to something that is not we, which means annihilation? or to something that is more we, which means a farther development of the original idea of us, the divine germ of us, holding in it all we ever were, all we ever can and must become? What is it constitutes this or that man? Is it what he himself thinks he is? Assuredly not. Is it what his friends at any given moment think him? Far from it. In which of his changing moods is he more himself? Loves any lover so little as to desire *no* change in the person loved—no something different to bring him or her closer to the indwelling ideal? In the loveliest is there not something not like her—something less lovely than she—some little thing in which a change would make her, not less, but more herself? Is it not of the very essence of the Christian hope, that we shall be changed from much bad to all good? If a wife so love that she would keep every opposition, every inconsistency in her husband's as yet but partially harmonious character, she does not love well enough for the kingdom of heaven. If its imperfections be essential to the individuality she loves, and to the repossession of her joy in it, she may be sure that, if he were restored to her as she would have him, she would soon come to love him less—perhaps to love him not at all; for no one who does not love perfection, will ever keep constant in loving. Fault is not lovable; it is only the good in which the alien fault dwells that causes it to seem capable of being loved. Neither is it any man's peculiarities that make him beloved; it is the essential humanity underlying those peculiarities. They may make him interesting, and, where not offensive, they may come to be loved for the sake of the man; but in themselves they are of smallest account.

We must not however confound peculiarity with diversity. Diversity is in and from God; peculiarity in and from man. The real man is the divine idea of him; the man God had in view when he began to send him forth out of thought into thinking; the man he is now working to perfect by casting out what is not he, and developing what is he. But in God's real men, that is, his ideal men, the diversity is infinite; he does not repeat his creations; every one of his children differs from every other, and in every one the diversity is lovable. God gives in his children an analysis of himself, an analysis that will never be exhausted. It is the original God-idea of the individual man that will at length be given, without spot or blemish, into the arms of love.

Such, surely, is the heart of the comfort the Lord will give those whose love is now making them mourn; and their present blessedness must be the expectation of the time when the true lover shall find the restored the same as the lost—with precious differences: the things that were not like the true self, gone or going; the things that were loveliest, lovelier still; the restored not merely more than the lost, but more the person lost than he or she that was lost. For the things which made him or her what he or she was, the things that rendered lovable, the things essential to the person, will be more present, because more developed.

Whether or not the Lord was here thinking specially of the mourners for the dead, as I think he was, he surely does not limit the word of comfort to them, or wish us to believe less than that his father has perfect comfort for every human grief. Out upon such miserable theologians as, instead of receiving them into the good soil of a generous heart, to bring forth truth an hundred fold, so cut and pare the words of the Lord as to take the very life from them, quenching all their glory and colour in their own inability to believe, and still would have the dead letter of them accepted as the comfort of a creator to the sore hearts he made in his own image! Here, 'as if they were God's spies,' some such would tell us that the Lord proclaims the blessedness of those that mourn for their sins, and of them only. What mere honest man would make a promise which was all a reservation, except in one unmentioned point! Assuredly they who mourn for their sins will be gloriously comforted, but certainly such also as are bowed down with any grief. The Lord would have us know that sorrow is not a part of life; that it is but a wind blowing throughout it, to winnow and cleanse. Where shall the woman go whose child is at the point of death, or whom the husband of her youth has forsaken, but to her Father in heaven? Must she keep away until she knows herself sorry for her sins? How should that woman care to be delivered from her sins, how could she accept any comfort, who believed the child of her bosom lost to her for ever? Would the Lord have such a one be of good cheer, of merry heart, because her sins were forgiven her? Would such a mother be a woman of whom the saviour of men might have been born? If a woman forget the child she has borne and nourished, how shall she remember the father from whom she has herself come? The Lord came to heal the broken-hearted; therefore he said, 'Blessed are the mourners.' Hope in God, mother, for the deadest of thy children, even for him who died in his sins. Thou mayest have long to wait for him—but he will be found. It may be, thou thyself wilt one day be sent to seek him and find him. Rest thy hope on no excuse thy love would make for him, neither upon any quibble theological or sacerdotal; hope on in him who created him, and who loves him more than thou. God will excuse him better than thou, and his uncovenanted mercy is larger than that of his ministers. Shall not *the* Father do *his* best to find his prodigal? the good shepherd to find his lost sheep? The angels in his presence know the Father, and watch for the prodigal. Thou shalt be comforted.

There is one phase of our mourning for the dead which I must not leave unconsidered, seeing it is the pain within pain of all our mourning—the sorrow, namely, with its keen recurrent pangs because of things we have said or done, or omitted to say or do, while we companied with the departed. The very life that would give itself to the other, aches with the sense of having, this time and that, not given what it might. We cast ourselves at their feet, crying, Forgive me, my heart's own! but they are pale with distance, and do not seem to hear. It may be that they are longing in like agony of love after us, but know better, or perhaps only are more assured than we, that we shall be comforted together by and by.

Bethink thee, brother, sister, I say; bethink thee of the splendour of God, and answer—Would he be perfect if in his restitution of all things there were no opportunity for declaring our bitter grief and shame for the past? no moment in which to sob—Sister, brother, I am thy slave? no room for making amends? At the same time, when the desired moment comes, one look in the eyes may be enough, and we shall know one another even as God knows us. Like the purposed words of the prodigal in the parable, it may be that the words of our confession will hardly find place. Heart may so speak to heart as to forget there were such things. Mourner, hope in God, and comfort where thou canst, and the lord of mourners will be able to comfort thee the sooner. It may be thy very severity with thyself, has already moved the Lord to take thy part.

Such as mourn the loss of love, such from whom the friend, the brother, the lover, has turned away—what shall I cry to them?—You too shall be comforted—only hearken: Whatever selfishness clouds the love that mourns the loss of love, that selfishness must be taken out of it—burned out of it even by pain extreme, if such be needful. By cause of that in thy love which was not love, it may be thy loss has come; anyhow, because of thy love's defect, thou must suffer that it may be supplied. God will not, like the unjust judge, avenge thee to escape the cry that troubles him. No crying will make him comfort thy selfishness. He will not render thee incapable of loving truly. He despises neither thy love though mingled with selfishness, nor thy suffering that springs from both; he will disentangle thy selfishness from thy love, and cast it into the fire. His cure for thy selfishness at once and thy suffering, is to make thee love more—and more truly; not with the love of love, but with the love of the person whose lost love thou bemoanest. For the love of love is the love of thyself. Begin to love as God loves, and thy grief will assuage; but for comfort wait his time. What he will do for thee, he only knows. It may be thou wilt never know what he will do, but only what he has done: it was too good for thee to know save by receiving it. The moment thou art capable of it, thine it will be.

One thing is clear in regard to every trouble—that the natural way with it is straight to the Father's knee. The Father is father *for* his children, else why did he make himself their father? Wouldst thou not, mourner, be comforted rather after the one eternal fashion—the child by the father—than in such poor temporary way as would but leave thee the more exposed to thy worst enemy, thine own unreclaimed self?—an enemy who has but this one good thing in him—that he will always bring thee to sorrow!

The Lord has come to wipe away our tears. He is doing it; he will have it done as soon as he can; and until he can, he would have them flow without bitterness; to which end he tells us it is a blessed thing to mourn, because of the comfort on its way. Accept his comfort now, and so prepare for the comfort at hand. He is getting you ready for it, but you must be a fellow worker with him, or he will never have done. He *must* have you pure in heart, eager after righteousness, a very child of his father in heaven.

*GOD'S FAMILY.*

'Blessed are the pure in heart, for they shall see God.' 'Blessed are they which do hunger and thirst after righteousness, for they shall be filled.' 'Blessed are the peace-makers, for they shall be called the children of God.'—*Matthew* v. 8, 6, 9.

The cry of the deepest in man has always been, to see God. It was the cry of Moses and the cry of Job, the cry of psalmist and of prophet; and to the cry, there has ever been faintly heard a far approach of coming answer. In the fullness of time the Son appears with the proclamation that a certain class of men shall behold the Father: 'Blessed are the pure in heart,' he cries, 'for they shall see God.' He who saw God, who sees him now, who always did and always will see him, says, 'Be pure, and you also shall see him.' To see God was the Lord's own, eternal, one happiness; therefore he knew that the essential bliss of the creature is to behold the face of the creator. In that face lies the mystery of a man's own nature, the history of a man's own being. He who can read no line of it, can know neither himself nor his fellow; he only who knows God a little, can at all understand man. The blessed in Dante's Paradise ever and always read each other's thoughts in God. Looking to him, they find their neighbour. All that the creature needs to see or know, all that the creature can see or know, is the face of him from whom he came. Not seeing and knowing it, he will never be at rest; seeing and knowing it, his existence will yet indeed be a mystery to him and an awe, but no more a dismay. To know that it is, and that it has power neither to continue nor to cease, must to any soul alive enough to appreciate the fact, be merest terror, save also it knows one with it the Power by which it exists. From the man who comes to know and feel that Power in him and one with him, loneliness, anxiety, and fear vanish; he is no more an orphan without a home, a little one astray on the cold waste of a helpless consciousness. 'Father,' he cries, 'hold me fast to thy creating will, that I may know myself one with it, know myself its outcome, its willed embodiment, and rejoice without trembling. Be this the delight of my being, that thou hast willed, hast loved me forth; let me know that I am thy child, born to obey thee. Dost thou not justify thy deed to thyself by thy tenderness toward me? dost thou not justify it to thy child by revealing to him his claim on thee because of thy disparture of him from thyself, because of his utter dependence on thee? Father, thou art in me, else I could not be in thee, could have no house for my soul to dwell in, or any world in which to walk abroad,'

These truths are, I believe, the very necessities of fact, but a man does not therefore, at a given moment, necessarily know them. It is absolutely necessary, none the less, to his real being, that he should know these spiritual relations in which he stands to his Origin; yea, that they should be always present and potent with him, and become the heart and sphere and all-pervading substance of his consciousness, of which they are the ground and foundation. Once to have seen them, is not always to see them. There are times, and those times many, when the cares of this world—with no right to any part in our thought, seeing either they are unreasonable or God imperfect—so blind the eyes of the soul to the radiance of the eternally true, that they see it only as if it ought to be true, not as if it must be true; as if it might be true in the region of thought, but could not be true in the region of fact. Our very senses, filled with the things of our passing sojourn, combine to cast discredit upon the existence of any world for the sake of which we are furnished with an inner eye, an eternal ear. But had we once seen God face to face, should we not be always and for ever sure of him? we have had but glimpses of the Father. Yet, if we had seen God face to face, but had again become impure of heart—if such a fearful thought be a possible idea— we should then no more believe that we had ever beheld him. A sin-beclouded soul could never recall the vision whose essential verity was its only possible proof. None but the pure in heart see God; only the growing-pure hope to see him. Even those who saw the Lord, the express image of his person, did not see God. They only saw Jesus—and then but the outside Jesus, or a little more. They were not pure in heart; they saw him and did not see him. They saw him with their eyes, but not with those eyes which alone can see God. Those were not born in them yet. Neither the eyes of the resurrection-body, nor the eyes of unembodied spirits can see God; only the eyes of that eternal something that is of the very essence of God, the thought-eyes, the truth-eyes, the love-eyes, can see him. It is not because we are created and he uncreated, it is not because of any difference involved in that difference of all differences, that we cannot see him. If he pleased to take a shape, and that shape were presented to us, and we saw that shape, we should not therefore be seeing God. Even if we knew it was a shape of God—call it even God himself our eyes rested upon; if we had been told the fact and believed the report; yet, if we did not see the *Godness*, were not capable of recognizing him, so as without the report to know the vision him, we should not be seeing God, we should only be seeing the tabernacle in which for the moment he dwelt. In other words, not seeing what in the form made it a form fit for him to take, we should not be seeing a presence which could only be God.

To see God is to stand on the highest point of created being. Not until we see God— no partial and passing embodiment of him, but the abiding presence—do we stand upon our own mountain-top, the height of the existence God has given us, and up to which he is leading us. That there we should stand, is the end of our creation. This truth is at the heart of everything, means all kinds of completions, may be uttered in many ways; but language will never compass it, for form will never contain it. Nor shall we ever see, that is know God perfectly. We shall indeed never absolutely know man or woman or child; but we may know God as we never can know human being—as we never can know ourselves. We not only may, but we must so know him, and it can never be until we are pure in heart. Then shall we know him with the infinitude of an ever-growing knowledge.

'What is it, then, to be pure in heart?'

I answer, It is not necessary to define this purity, or to have in the mind any clear form of it. For even to know perfectly, were that possible, what purity of heart is, would not be to be pure in heart.

'How then am I to try after it? can I do so without knowing what it is?'

Though you do not know any definition of purity, you know enough to begin to be pure. You do not know what a man is, but you know how to make his acquaintance—perhaps even how to gain his friendship. Your brain does not know what purity is; your heart has some acquaintance with purity itself. Your brain in seeking to know what it is, may even obstruct your heart in bettering its friendship with it. To know what purity is, a man must already be pure; but he who can put the question, already knows enough of purity, I repeat, to begin to become pure. If this moment you determine to start for purity, your conscience will at once tell you where to begin. If you reply, 'My conscience says nothing definite'; I answer, 'You are but playing with your conscience. Determine, and it will speak.'

If you care to see God, be pure. If you will not be pure, you will grow more and more impure; and instead of seeing God, will at length find yourself face to face with a vast inane—a vast inane, yet filled full of one inhabitant, that devouring monster, your own false self. If for this neither do you care, I tell you there is a Power that will not have it so; a Love that will make you care by the consequences of not caring.

You who seek purity, and would have your fellow-men also seek it, spend not your labour on the stony ground of their intellect, endeavouring to explain what purity is; give their imagination the one pure man; call up their conscience to witness against their own deeds; urge upon them the grand resolve to be pure. With the first endeavour of a soul toward her, Purity will begin to draw nigh, calling for admittance; and never will a man have to pause in the divine toil, asking what next is required of him; the demands of the indwelling Purity will ever be in front of his slow-labouring obedience.

If one should say, 'Alas, I am shut out from this blessing! I am not pure in heart: never shall I see God!' here is another word from the same eternal heart to comfort him, making his grief its own consolation. For this man also there is blessing with the messenger of the Father. Unhappy men were we, if God were the God of the perfected only, and not of the growing, the becoming! 'Blessed are they,' says the Lord, concerning the not yet pure, 'which do hunger and thirst after righteousness, for they shall be filled.' Filled with righteousness, they are pure; pure, they shall see God.

Long ere the Lord appeared, ever since man was on the earth, nay, surely, from the very beginning, was his spirit at work in it for righteousness; in the fullness of time he came in his own human person, to fulfil all righteousness. He came to his own of the same mind with himself, who hungered and thirsted after righteousness. They should be fulfilled of righteousness!

To hunger and thirst after anything, implies a sore personal need, a strong desire, a passion for that thing. Those that hunger and thirst after righteousness, seek with their whole nature the design of that nature. Nothing less will give them satisfaction; that alone will set them at ease. They long to be delivered from their sins, to send them away, to be clean and blessed by their absence—in a word to become men, God's men; for, sin gone, all the rest is good. It was not in such hearts, it was not in any heart that the revolting legal fiction of imputed righteousness arose. Righteousness itself, God's righteousness, rightness in their own being, in heart and brain and hands, is what they desire. Of such men was Nathanael, in whom was no guile; such, perhaps, was Nicodemus too, although he did come to Jesus by night; such was Zacchaeus. The temple could do nothing to deliver them; but, by their very futility, its observances had done their work, developing the desires they could not meet, making the men hunger and thirst the more after genuine righteousness: the Lord must bring them this bread from heaven. With him, the live, original rightness, in their hearts, they must speedily become righteous. With that Love their friend, who is at once both the root and the flower of things, they would strive vigorously as well as hunger eagerly after righteousness. Love is the father of righteousness. It could not be, and could not be hungered after, but for love. The lord of righteousness himself could not live without Love, without the Father in him. Every heart was created for, and can live no otherwise than in and upon love eternal, perfect, pure, unchanging; and love necessitates righteousness. In how many souls has not the very thought of a real God waked a longing to be different, to be pure, to be right! The fact that this feeling is possible, that a soul can become dissatisfied with itself, and desire a change in itself, reveals God as an essential part of its being; for in itself the soul is aware that it cannot be what it would, what it ought—that it cannot set itself right: a need has been generated in the soul for which the soul can generate no supply; a presence higher than itself must have caused that need; a power greater than itself must supply it, for the soul knows its very need, its very lack, is of something greater than itself.

But the primal need of the human soul is yet greater than this; the longing after righteousness is only one of the manifestations of it; the need itself is that of *existence not self-existent* for the consciousness of the presence of the causing Self-existent. It is the man's need of God. A moral, that is, a human, a spiritual being, must either be God, or one with God. This truth begins to reveal itself when the man begins to feel that he cannot cast out the thing he hates, cannot be the thing he loves.

That he hates thus, that he loves thus, is because God is in him, but he finds he has not enough of God. His awaking strength manifests itself in his sense of weakness, for only strength can know itself weak. The negative cannot know itself at all. Weakness cannot know itself weak. It is a little strength that longs for more; it is infant righteousness that hungers after righteousness.

To every soul dissatisfied with itself, comes this word, at once rousing and consoling, from the Power that lives and makes him live—that in his hungering and thirsting he is blessed, for he shall be filled. His hungering and thirsting is the divine pledge of the divine meal. The more he hungers and thirsts the more blessed is he; the more room is there in him to receive that which God is yet more eager to give than he to have. It is the miserable emptiness that makes a man hunger and thirst; and, as the body, so the soul hungers after what belongs to its nature. A man hungers and thirsts after righteousness because his nature needs it—needs it because it was made for it; his soul desires its own. His nature is good, and desires more good. Therefore, that he is empty of good, needs discourage no one; for what is emptiness but room to be filled? Emptiness is need of good; the emptiness that desires good, is itself good. Even if the hunger after righteousness should in part spring from a desire after self-respect, it is not therefore *all* false. A man could not even be ashamed of himself, without some 'feeling sense' of the beauty of rightness. By divine degrees the man will at length grow sick of himself, and desire righteousness with a pure hunger—just as a man longs to eat that which is good, nor thinks of the strength it will restore.

To be filled with righteousness, will be to forget even righteousness itself in the bliss of being righteous, that is, a child of God. The thought of righteousness will vanish in the fact of righteousness. When a creature is just what he is meant to be, what only he is fit to be; when, therefore, he is truly himself, he never thinks what he is. He *is* that thing; why think about it? It is no longer outside of him that he should contemplate or desire it.

God made man, and woke in him the hunger for righteousness; the Lord came to enlarge and rouse this hunger. The first and lasting effect of his words must be to make the hungering and thirsting long yet more. If their passion grow to a despairing sense of the unattainable, a hopelessness of ever gaining that without which life were worthless, let them remember that the Lord congratulates the hungry and thirsty, so sure does he know them of being one day satisfied. Their hunger is a precious thing to have, none the less that it were a bad thing to retain unappeased. It springs from the lack but also from the love of good, and its presence makes it possible to supply the lack. Happy, then, ye pining souls! The food you would have, is the one thing the Lord would have you have, the very thing he came to bring you! Fear not, ye hungering and thirsting; you shall have righteousness enough, though none to spare—none to spare, yet enough to overflow upon every man. See how the Lord goes on filling his disciples, John and Peter and James and Paul, with righteousness from within! What honest soul, interpreting the servant by the master, and unbiassed by the tradition of them that would shut the kingdom of heaven against men, can doubt what Paul means by 'the righteousness which is of God by faith'? He was taught of Jesus Christ through the words he had spoken; and the man who does not understand Jesus Christ, will never understand his apostles. What righteousness could St Paul have meant but the same the Lord would have men hunger and thirst after—the very righteousness wherewith God is righteous! They that hunger and thirst after such only righteousness, shall become pure in heart, and shall see God.

If your hunger seems long in being filled, it is well it should seem long. But what if your righteousness tarry, because your hunger after it is not eager? There are who sit long at the table because their desire is slow; they eat as who should say, We need no food. In things spiritual, increasing desire is the sign that satisfaction is drawing nearer. But it were better to hunger after righteousness for ever than to dull the sense of lack with the husks of the Christian scribes and lawyers: he who trusts in the atonement instead of in the father of Jesus Christ, fills his fancy with the chimeras of a vulgar legalism, not his heart with the righteousness of God.

Hear another like word of the Lord. He assures us that the Father hears the cries of his elect—of those whom he seeks to worship him because they worship in spirit and in truth. 'Shall not God avenge his own elect,' he says, 'which cry day and night unto him?' Now what can God's elect have to keep on crying for, night and day, but righteousness? He allows that God seems to put off answering them, but assures us he will answer them speedily. Even now he must be busy answering their prayers; increasing hunger is the best possible indication that he is doing so. For some divine reason it is well they should not yet know in themselves that he is answering their prayers; but the day must come when we shall be righteous even as he is righteous; when no word of his will miss being understood because of our lack of righteousness; when no unrighteousness shall hide from our eyes the face of the Father.

These two promises, of seeing God, and being filled with righteousness, have place between the individual man and his father in heaven directly; the promise I now come to, has place between a man and his God as the God of other men also, as the father of the whole family in heaven and earth: 'Blessed are the peace-makers, for they shall be called the children of God.'

Those that are on their way to see God, those who are growing pure in heart through hunger and thirst after righteousness, are indeed the children of God; but specially the Lord calls those his children who, on their way home, are peace-makers in the travelling company; for, surely, those in any family are specially the children, who make peace with and among the rest. The true idea of the universe is the whole family in heaven and earth. All the children in this part of it, the earth, at least, are not good children; but however far, therefore, the earth is from being a true portion of a real family, the life-germ at the root of the world, that by and for which it exists, is its relation to God the father of men. For the development of this germ in the consciousness of the children, the church—whose idea is the purer family within the more mixed, ever growing as leaven within the meal by absorption, but which itself is, alas! not easily distinguishable from the world it would change—is one of the passing means. For the same purpose, the whole divine family is made up of numberless human families, that in these, men may learn and begin to love one another. God, then, would make of the world a true, divine family. Now the primary necessity to the very existence of a family is peace. Many a human family is no family, and the world is no family yet, for the lack of peace. Wherever peace is growing, there of course is the live peace, counteracting disruption and disintegration, and helping the development of the true essential family. The one question, therefore, as to any family is, whether peace or strife be on the increase in it; for peace alone makes it possible for the binding grass-roots of life—love, namely, and justice—to spread throughout what were else but a wind-blown heap of still drifting sand. The peace-makers quiet the winds of the world ever ready to be up and blowing; they tend and cherish the interlacing roots of the ministering grass; they spin and twist many uniting cords, and they weave many supporting bands; they are the servants, for the truth's sake, of the individual, of the family, of the world, of the great universal family of heaven and earth. They are the true children of that family, the allies and ministers of every clasping and consolidating force in it; fellow-workers they are with God in the creation of the family; they help him to get it to his mind, to perfect his father-idea. Ever radiating peace, they welcome love, but do not seek it; they provoke no jealousy. They are the children of God, for like him they would be one with his creatures. His eldest son, his very likeness, was the first of the family-peace-makers. Preaching peace to them that were afar off and them that were nigh, he stood undefended in the turbulent crowd of his fellows, and it was only over his dead body that his brothers began to come together in the peace that will not be broken. He rose again from the dead; his peace-making brothers, like himself, are dying unto sin; and not yet have the evil children made their father hate, or their elder brother flinch.

On the other hand, those whose influence is to divide and separate, causing the hearts of men to lean away from each other, make themselves the children of the evil one: born of God and not of the devil, they turn from God, and adopt the devil their father. They set their God-born life against God, against the whole creative, redemptive purpose of his unifying will, ever obstructing the one prayer of the first-born—that the children may be one with him in the Father. Against the heart-end of creation, against that for which the Son yielded himself utterly, the sowers of strife, the fomenters of discord, contend ceaseless. They do their part with all the other powers of evil to make the world which the love of God holds together—a world at least, though not yet a family—one heaving mass of dissolution. But they labour in vain. Through the mass and through it, that it may cohere, this way and that, guided in dance inexplicable of prophetic harmony, move the children of God, the lights of the world, the lovers of men, the fellow-workers with God, the peace-makers—ever weaving, after a pattern devised by, and known only to him who orders their ways, the web of the world's history. But for them the world would have no history; it would vanish, a cloud of windborne dust. As in his labour, so shall these share in the joy of God, in the divine fruition of victorious endeavour. Blessed are the peace-makers, for they shall be called the children of God—*the* children because they set the Father on the throne of the Family.

The main practical difficulty, with some at least of the peace-makers, is, how to carry themselves toward the undoers of peace, the disuniters of souls. Perhaps the most potent of these are not those powers of the church visible who care for canon and dogma more than for truth, and for the church more than for Christ; who take uniformity for unity; who strain at a gnat and swallow a camel, nor knowing what spirit they are of; such men, I say, are perhaps neither the most active nor the most potent force working for the disintegration of the body of Christ. I imagine also that neither are the party-liars of politics the worst foes to divine unity, ungenerous, and often knowingly false as they are to their opponents, to whom they seem to have no desire to be honest and fair. I think, rather, they must be the babbling liars of the social circle, and the faithless brothers and unloving sisters of disunited human families. But why inquire? Every self-assertion, every form of self-seeking however small or poor, world-noble or grotesque, is a separating and scattering force. And these forces are multitudinous, these points of radial repulsion are innumerable, because of the prevailing passion of mean souls to seem great, and feel important. If such cannot hope to attract the attention of the great-little world, if they cannot even become 'the cynosure of neighbouring eyes,' they will, in what sphere they may call their own, however small it be, try to make a party for themselves; each, revolving on his or her own axis, will attempt to self-centre a private whirlpool of human monads. To draw such a surrounding, the partisan of self will sometimes gnaw asunder the most precious of bonds, poison whole broods of infant loves. Such real schismatics go about, where not inventing evil, yet rejoicing in iniquity; mishearing; misrepresenting; paralyzing affection; separating hearts. Their chosen calling is that of the strife-maker, the child of the dividing devil. They belong to the class of *the perfidious*, whom Dante places in the lowest infernal gulf as their proper home. Many a woman who now imagines herself standing well in morals and religion, will find herself at last just such a child of the devil; and her misery will be the hope of her redemption.

But it is not for her sake that I write these things: would such a woman recognize her own likeness, were I to set it down as close as words could draw it? I am rather as one groping after some light on the true behaviour toward her kind. Are we to treat persons known for liars and strife-makers as the children of the devil or not? Are we to turn away from them, and refuse to acknowledge them, rousing an ignorant strife of tongues concerning our conduct? Are we guilty of connivance, when silent as to the ambush whence we know the wicked arrow privily shot? Are we to call the traitor to account? or are we to give warning of any sort? I have no answer. Each must carry the question that perplexes to the Light of the World. To what purpose is the spirit of God promised to them that ask it, if not to help them order their way aright?

One thing is plain—that we must love the strife-maker; another is nearly as plain—-that, if we do not love him, we must leave him alone; for without love there can be no peace-making, and words will but occasion more strife. To be kind neither hurts nor compromises. Kindness has many phases, and the fitting form of it may avoid offence, and must avoid untruth.

We must not fear what man can do to us, but commit our way to the Father of the Family. We must be nowise anxious to defend ourselves; and if not ourselves because God is our defence, then why our friends? is he not their defence as much as ours? Commit thy friend's cause also to him who judgeth righteously. Be ready to bear testimony for thy friend, as thou wouldst to receive the blow struck at him; but do not plunge into a nest of scorpions to rescue his handkerchief. Be true to him thyself, nor spare to show thou lovest and honourest him; but defence may dishonour: men may say, What! is thy friend's esteem then so small? He is unwise who drags a rich veil from a cactus-bush.

Whatever our relation, then, with any peace-breaker, our mercy must ever be within call; and it may help us against an indignation too strong to be pure, to remember that when any man is reviled for righteousness-sake, then is he blessed.

*THE REWARD OF OBEDIENCE.*

'Blessed are the merciful, for they shall obtain mercy.' 'Blessed are they which are persecuted for righteousness' sake, for theirs is the kingdom of heaven. Blessed are ye when men shall revile you and persecute you, and shall say all manner of evil against you falsely, for my sake. Rejoice and be exceeding glad, for great is your reward in heaven; for so persecuted they the prophets which were before you.'— *Matthew*, v. 7, 10 11, 12.

Mercy cannot get in where mercy goes not out. The outgoing makes way for the incoming. God takes the part of humanity against the man. The man must treat men as he would have God treat him. 'If ye forgive men their trespasses,' the Lord says, 'your heavenly father will also forgive you; but if ye forgive not men their trespasses, neither will your father forgive your trespasses. And in the prophecy of the judgment of the Son of man, he represents himself as saying, 'Inasmuch as ye have done it unto one of the least of these my brethren, ye have done it unto me.'

But the demand for mercy is far from being for the sake only of the man who needs his neighbour's mercy; it is greatly more for the sake of the man who must show the mercy. It is a small thing to a man whether or not his neighbour be merciful to him; it is life or death to him whether or not he be merciful to his neighbour. The greatest mercy that can be shown to man, is to make him merciful; therefore, if he will not be merciful, the mercy of God must compel him thereto. In the parable of the king taking account of his servants, he delivers the unmerciful debtor to the tormentors, 'till he should pay all that was due unto him.' The king had forgiven his debtor, but as the debtor refuses to pass on the forgiveness to his neighbour—the only way to make a return in kind—the king withdraws his forgiveness. If we forgive not men their trespasses, our trespasses remain. For how can God in any sense forgive, remit, or send away the sin which a man insists on retaining? Unmerciful, we must be given up to the tormentors until we learn to be merciful. God is merciful: we must be merciful. There is no blessedness except in being such as God; it would be altogether unmerciful to leave us unmerciful. The reward of the merciful is, that by their mercy they are rendered capable of receiving the mercy of God—yea, God himself, who is Mercy.

That men may be drawn to taste and see and understand, the Lord associates reward with righteousness. The Lord would have men love righteousness, but how are they to love it without being acquainted with it? How are they to go on loving it without a growing knowledge of it? To draw them toward it that they may begin to know it, and to encourage them when assailed by the disappointments that accompany endeavour, he tells them simply a truth concerning it—that in the doing of it, there is great reward. Let no one start with dismay at the idea of a reward of righteousness, saying virtue is its own reward. Is not virtue then a reward? Is any other imaginable reward worth mentioning beside it? True, the man may, after this mode or that, mistake the reward promised; not the less must he have it, or perish. Who will count himself deceived by overfulfilment? Would a parent be deceiving his child in saying, 'My boy, you will have a great reward if you learn Greek,' foreseeing his son's delight in Homer and Plato—now but a valueless waste in his eyes? When his reward comes, will the youth feel aggrieved that it is Greek, and not bank-notes?

The nature indeed of the Lord's promised rewards is hardly to be mistaken; yet the foolish remarks one sometimes hears, make me wish to point out that neither is the Lord proclaiming an ethical system, nor does he make the blunder of representing as righteousness the doing of a good thing because of some advantage to be thereby gained. When he promises, he only states some fact that will encourage his disciples—that is, all who learn of him—to meet the difficulties in the way of doing right and so learning righteousness, his object being to make men righteous, not to teach them philosophy. I doubt if those who would, on the ground of mentioned reward, set aside the teaching of the Lord, are as anxious to be righteous as they are to prove him unrighteous. If they were, they would, I think, take more care to represent him truly; they would make farther search into the thing, nor be willing that he whom the world confesses its best man, and whom they themselves, perhaps, confess their superior in conduct, should be found less pure in theory than they. Must the Lord hide from his friends that they will have cause to rejoice that they have been obedient? Must he give them no help to counterbalance the load with which they start on their race? Is he to tell them the horrors of the persecutions that await them, and not the sweet sympathies that will help them through? Was it wrong to assure them that where he was going they should go also? The Lord could not demand of them more righteousness than he does: 'Be ye therefore perfect as your father in heaven is perfect;' but not to help them by word of love, deed of power, and promise of good, would have shown him far less of a brother and a saviour. It is the part of the enemy of righteousness to increase the difficulties in the way of becoming righteous, and to diminish those in the way of seeming righteous. Jesus desires no righteousness for the pride of being righteous, any more than for advantage to be gained by it; therefore, while requiring such purity as the man, beforehand, is unable to imagine, he gives him all the encouragement he can. He will not enhance his victory by difficulties—of them there are enough—but by completeness. He will not demand the loftiest motives in the yet far from loftiest soul: to those the soul must grow. He will hearten the child with promises, and fulfil them to the contentment of the man.

Men cannot be righteous without love; to love a righteous man is the best, the only way to learn righteousness: the Lord gives us himself to love, and promises his closest friendship to them that overcome.

God's rewards are always in kind. 'I am your father; be my children, and I will be your father.' Every obedience is the opening of another door into the boundless universe of life. So long as the constitution of that universe remains, so long as the world continues to be made by God, righteousness can never fail of perfect reward. Before it could be otherwise, the government must have passed into other hands.

The idea of merit is nowise essential to that of reward. Jesus tells us that the lord who finds his servant faithful, will make him sit down to meat, and come forth and serve him; he says likewise, 'When ye have done all, say we are unprofitable servants; we have done only that which it was our duty to do.' Reward is the rebound of Virtue's well-served ball from the hand of Love; a sense of merit is the most sneaking shape that self-satisfaction can assume. God's reward lies closed in all well-doing: the doer of right grows better and humbler, and comes nearer to God's heart as nearer to his likeness; grows more capable of God's own blessedness, and of inheriting the kingdoms of heaven and earth. To be made greater than one's fellows is the offered reward of hell, and involves no greatness; to be made greater than one's self, is the divine reward, and involves a real greatness. A man might be set above all his fellows, to be but so much less than he was before; a man cannot be raised a hair's-breadth above himself, without rising nearer to God. The reward itself, then, is righteousness; and the man who was righteous for the sake of such reward, knowing what it was, would be righteous for the sake of righteousness,—which yet, however, would not be perfection. But I must distinguish and divide no farther now.

The reward of mercy is not often of this world; the merciful do not often receive mercy in return from their fellows; perhaps they do not often receive much gratitude. None the less, being the children of their father in heaven, will they go on to show mercy, even to their enemies. They must give like God, and like God be blessed in giving.

There is a mercy that lies in the endeavour to share with others the best things God has given: they who do so will be persecuted, and reviled, and slandered, as well as thanked and loved and befriended. The Lord not only promises the greatest possible reward; he tells his disciples the worst they have to expect. He not only shows them the fair countries to which they are bound; he tells them the truth of the rough weather and the hardships of the way. He will not have them choose in ignorance. At the same time he strengthens them to meet coming difficulty, by instructing them in its real nature. All this is part of his preparation of them for his work, for taking his yoke upon them, and becoming fellow-labourers with him in his father's vineyard. They must not imagine, because they are the servants of his father, that therefore they shall find their work easy; they shall only find the reward great. Neither will he have them fancy, when evil comes upon them, that something unforeseen, unprovided for, has befallen them. It is just then, on the contrary, that their reward comes nigh: when men revile them and persecute them, then they may know that they are blessed. Their suffering is ground for rejoicing, for exceeding gladness. The ignominy cast upon them leaves the name of the Lord's Father written upon their foreheads, the mark of the true among the false, of the children among the slaves. With all who suffer for the world, persecution is the seal of their patent, a sign that they were sent: they fill up that which is behind of the afflictions of Christ for his body's sake.

Let us look at the similar words the Lord spoke in a later address to his disciples, in the presence of thousands, on the plain,—supplemented with lamentation over such as have what they desire: St Luke vi. 20—26.

*'Blessed be ye poor, for yours is the kingdom of God. Blessed are ye that hunger now, for ye shall be filled. Blessed are ye that weep now, for ye shall laugh. Blessed are ye when men shall hate you, and when they shall separate you from their company, and shall reproach you, and cast out your name as evil, for the Son of Man's sake. Rejoice ye in that day, and leap for joy, for behold your reward is great in heaven; for in the like manner did their fathers unto the prophets.*

*'But woe unto you that are rich! for ye have received your consolation. Woe unto you that are full, for ye shall hunger. Woe unto you that laugh now, for ye shall mourn and weep. Woe unto you when all men shall speak well of you; for so did their fathers to the false prophets.'*

On this occasion he uses the word *hunger* without limitation. Every true want, every genuine need, every God-created hunger, is a thing provided for in the idea of the universe; but no attempt to fill a void otherwise than the Heart of the Universe intended and intends, is or can be anything but a woe. God forgets none of his children—the naughty ones any more than the good. Love and reward is for the good: love and correction for the bad. The bad ones will trouble the good, but shall do them no hurt. The evil a man does to his neighbour, shall do his neighbour no harm, shall work indeed for his good; but he himself will have to mourn for his doing. A sore injury to himself, it is to his neighbour a cause of jubilation—not for the evil the man does to himself—over that there is sorrow in heaven—but for the good it occasions his neighbour. The poor, the hungry, the weeping, the hated, may lament their lot as if God had forgotten them; but God is all the time caring for them. Blessed in his sight now, they shall soon know themselves blessed. 'Blessed are ye that weep now, for ye shall laugh.'—Welcome words from the glad heart of the Saviour! Do they not make our hearts burn within us?—They shall be comforted even to laughter! The poor, the hungry, the weeping, the hated, the persecuted, are the powerful, the opulent, the merry, the loved, the victorious of God's kingdom,—to be filled with good things, to laugh for very delight, to be honoured and sought and cherished!

But such as have their poor consolation in this life—alas for them!—for those who have yet to learn what hunger is! for those whose laughter is as the crackling of thorns! for those who have loved and gathered the praises of men! for the rich, the jocund, the full-fed! Silent-footed evil is on its way to seize them. Dives must go without; Lazarus must have. God's education makes use of terrible extremes. There are last that shall be first, and first that shall be last.

The Lord knew what trials, what tortures even awaited his disciples after his death; he knew they would need every encouragement he could give them to keep their hearts strong, lest in some moment of dismay they should deny him. If they had denied him, where would our gospel be? If there are none able and ready to be crucified for him now, alas for the age to come! What a poor travesty of the good news of God will arrive at their doors!

Those whom our Lord felicitates are all the children of one family; and everything that can be called blessed or blessing comes of the same righteousness. If a disciple be blessed because of any one thing, every other blessing is either his, or on the way to become his; for he is on the way to receive the very righteousness of God. Each good thing opens the door to the one next it, so to all the rest. But as if these his assurances and promises and comfortings were not large enough; as if the mention of any condition whatever might discourage some humble man of heart with a sense of unfitness, with the fear, perhaps conviction that the promise was not for him; as if some one might say, 'Alas, I am proud, and neither poor in spirit nor meek; I am at times not at all hungry after righteousness; I am not half merciful, and am very ready to feel hurt and indignant: I am shut out from every blessing!' the Lord, knowing the multitudes that can urge nothing in their own favour, and sorely feel they are not blessed, looks abroad over the wide world of his brothers and sisters, and calls aloud, including in the boundless invitation every living soul with but the one qualification of unrest or discomfort, 'Come unto me all ye that labour and are heavy laden, and I will give you rest.'

*THE YOKE OF JESUS.*

At that time Jesus answered and said,—according to Luke, In that hour Jesus rejoiced in spirit, and said,—'I thank thee, O Father, Lord of heaven and earth, because thou hast hid these things from the wise and prudent, and hast revealed them unto babes. Even so, Father, for so it seemed good in thy sight.

'All things are delivered unto me of my father; and no man knoweth the son,'—according to Luke, 'who the son is,'—'but the father; neither knoweth any man the father,'—according to Luke, 'who the father is,'—'save the son, and he to whomsoever the son will reveal him.'—*Matthew* xi. 25—27; *Luke* x. 21, 22.

'Come unto me, all ye that labour, and are heavy laden, and I will give you rest. Take my yoke upon you, and learn of me, for I am meek and lowly in heart; and ye shall find rest unto your souls. For my yoke is easy, and my burden is light.' *Matthew* xi. 28—30.

The words of the Lord in the former two of these paragraphs, are represented, both by Matthew and by Luke, as spoken after the denunciation of the cities of Chorazin,

Bethsaida, and Capernaum; only in Luke's narrative, the return of the seventy is mentioned between; and there the rejoicing of the Lord over the Father's revelation of himself to babes, appears to have reference to the seventy. The fact that the return of the seventy is not mentioned elsewhere, leaves us free to suppose that the words were indeed spoken on that occasion. The circumstances, however, as circumstances, are to us of little importance, not being necessary to the understanding of the words.

The Lord makes no complaint against the wise and prudent; he but recognizes that they are not those to whom his father reveals his best things; for which fact and the reasons of it, he thanks, or praises his father. 'I bless thy will: I see that thou art right: I am of one mind with thee:' something of each of these phases of meaning seems to belong to the Greek word.

'But why not reveal true things first to the wise? Are they not the fittest to receive them?' Yes, if these things and their wisdom lie in the same region—not otherwise. No amount of knowledge or skill in physical science, will make a man the fitter to argue a metaphysical question; and the wisdom of this world, meaning by the term, the philosophy of prudence, self-protection, precaution, specially unfits a man for receiving what the Father has to reveal: in proportion to our care about our own well being, is our incapability of understanding and welcoming the care of the Father. The wise and the prudent, with all their energy of thought, could never see the things of the Father sufficiently to recognize them as true. Their sagacity labours in earthly things, and so fills their minds with their own questions and conclusions, that they cannot see the eternal foundations God has laid in man, or the consequent necessities of their own nature. They are proud of finding out things, but the things they find out are all less than themselves. Because, however, they have discovered them, they imagine such things the goal of the human intellect. If they grant there may be things beyond those, they either count them beyond their reach, or declare themselves uninterested in them: for the wise and prudent, they do not exist. They work only to gather by the senses, and deduce from what they have so gathered, the prudential, the probable, the expedient, the protective. They never think of the essential, of what in itself must be. They are cautious, wary, discreet, judicious, circumspect, provident, temporizing. They have no enthusiasm, and are shy of all forms of it—a clever, hard, thin people, who take *things* for the universe, and love of facts for love of truth. They know nothing deeper in man than mere surface mental facts and their relations. They do not perceive, or they turn away from any truth which the intellect cannot formulate. Zeal for God will never eat them up: why should it? he is not interesting to them: theology may be; to such men religion means theology. How should the treasure of the Father be open to such? In their hands his rubies would draw in their fire, and cease to glow. The roses of paradise in their gardens would blow withered. They never go beyond the porch of the temple; they are not sure whether there be any *adytum*, and they do not care to go in and see: why indeed should they? it would but be to turn and come out again. Even when they know their duty, they must take it to pieces, and consider the grounds of its claim before they will render it obedience. All those evil doctrines about God that work misery and madness, have their origin in the brains of the wise and prudent, not in the hearts of the children. These wise and prudent, careful to make the words of his messengers rime with their conclusions, interpret the great heart of God, not by their own hearts, but by their miserable intellects; and, postponing the obedience which alone can give power to the understanding, press upon men's minds their wretched interpretations of the will of the Father, instead of the doing of that will upon their hearts. They call their philosophy the truth of God, and say men must hold it, or stand outside. They are the slaves of the letter in all its weakness and imperfection,—and will be until the spirit of the Word, the spirit of obedience shall set them free.

The babes must beware lest the wise and prudent come between them and the Father. They must yield no claim to authority over their belief, made by man or community, by church any more than by synagogue. That alone is for them to believe which the Lord reveals to their souls as true; that alone is it possible for them to believe with what he counts belief. The divine object for which teacher or church exists, is the persuasion of the individual heart to come to Jesus, the spirit, to be taught what he alone can teach.

Terribly has his gospel suffered in the mouths of the wise and prudent: how would it be faring now, had its first messages been committed to persons of repute, instead of those simple fishermen? It would be nowhere, or, if anywhere, unrecognizable. From the first we should have had a system founded on a human interpretation of the divine gospel, instead of the gospel itself, which would have disappeared. As it is, we have had one dull miserable human system after another usurping its place; but, thank God, the gospel remains! The little child, heedless of his trailing cloud of glory, and looking about him aghast in an unknown world, may yet see and run to the arms open to the children. How often has not some symbol employed in the New Testament been forced into the service of argument for one or another contemptible scheme of redemption, which were no redemption; while the truth for the sake of which the symbol was used, the thing meant to be conveyed by it, has lain unregarded beside the heap of rubbish! Had the wise and prudent been the confidants of God, I repeat, the letter would at once have usurped the place of the spirit; the ministering slave would have been set over the household; a system of religion, with its rickety, malodorous plan of salvation, would not only have at once been put in the place of a living Christ, but would yet have held that place. The great brother, the human God, the eternal Son, the living one, would have been as utterly hidden from the tearful eyes and aching hearts of the weary and heavy-laden, as if he had never come from the deeps of love to call the children home out of the shadows of a self-haunted universe. But the Father revealed the Father's things to his babes; the babes loved, and began to do them, therewith began to understand them, and went on growing in the knowledge of them and in the power of communicating them; while to the wise and prudent, the deepest words of the most babe-like of them all, John Boanerges, even now appear but a finger-worn rosary of platitudes. The babe understands the wise and prudent, but is understood only by the babe.

The Father, then, revealed his things to babes, because the babes were his own little ones, uncorrupted by the wisdom or the care of this world, and therefore able to receive them. The others, though his children, had not begun to be like him, therefore could not receive them. The Father's things could not have got anyhow into their minds without leaving all their value, all their spirit, outside the unchildlike place. The babes are near enough whence they come, to understand a little how things go in the presence of their father in heaven, and thereby to interpret the words of the Son. The child who has not yet 'walked above a mile or two from' his 'first love,' is not out of touch with the mind of his Father. Quickly will he seal the old bond when the Son himself, the first of the babes, the one perfect babe of God, comes to lead the children out of the lovely 'shadows of eternity' into the land of the 'white celestial thought.' As God is the one only real father, so is it only to God that any one can be a perfect child. In his garden only can childhood blossom.

The leader of the great array of little ones, himself, in virtue of his firstborn childhood, the first recipient of the revelations of his father, having thus given thanks, and said why he gave thanks, breaks out afresh, renewing expression of delight that God had willed it thus: 'Even so, father, for so it seemed good in thy sight!' I venture to translate, 'Yea, O Father, for thus came forth satisfaction before thee!' and think he meant, 'Yea, Father, for thereat were all thy angels filled with satisfaction,' The babes were the prophets in heaven, and the angels were glad to find it was to be so upon the earth also; they rejoiced to see that what was bound in heaven, was bound on earth; that the same principle held in each. Compare Matt, xviii. 10 and 14; also Luke xv. 10. 'See that ye despise not one of these little ones; for I say unto you that their angels in heaven do always behold the face of my father which is in heaven.... Thus it is not the will before your father which is in heaven,'—*among the angels who stand before him*, I think he means,—'that one of these little ones should perish.' 'Even so, I say unto you, there is joy in the presence of the angels of God over one sinner that repenteth.'

Having thus thanked his father that he has done after his own 'good and acceptable and perfect will', he turns to his disciples, and tells them that he knows the Father, being his Son, and that he only can reveal the Father to the rest of his children: 'All things are delivered unto me of my father; and no one knoweth the son but the father; neither knoweth any one the father save the son, and he to whomsoever the son willeth to reveal him.' It is almost as if his mention of the babes brought his thoughts back to himself and his father, between whom lay the secret of all life and all sending—yea, all loving. The relation of the Father and the Son contains the idea of the universe. Jesus tells his disciples that his father had no secrets from him; that he knew the Father as the Father knew him. The Son must know the Father; he only could know him—and knowing, he could reveal him; the Son could make the other, the imperfect children, know the Father, and so become such as he. All things were given unto him by the Father, because he was the Son of the Father: for the same reason he could reveal the things of the Father to the child of the Father. The child-relation is the one eternal, ever enduring, never changing relation.

Note that, while the Lord here represents the knowledge his father and he have each of the other as limited to themselves, the statement is one of fact only, not of design or intention: his presence in the world is for the removal of that limitation. The Father knows the Son and sends him to us that we may know him; the Son knows the

Father, and dies to reveal him. The glory of God's mysteries is—that they are for his children to look into.

When the Lord took the little child in the presence of his disciples, and declared him his representative, he made him the representative of his father also; but the eternal child alone can reveal him. To reveal is immeasurably more than to represent; it is to present to the eyes that know the true when they see it. Jesus represented God; the spirit of Jesus reveals God. The represented God a man may refuse; many refused the Lord; the revealed God no one can refuse; to see God and to love him are one. He can be revealed only to the child; perfectly, to the pure child only. All the discipline of the world is to make men children, that God may be revealed to them.

No man, when first he comes to himself, can have any true knowledge of God; he can only have a desire after such knowledge. But while he does not know him at all, he cannot become in his heart God's child; so the Father must draw nearer to him. He sends therefore his first born, who does know him, is exactly like him, and can represent him perfectly. Drawn to him, the children receive him, and then he is able to reveal the Father to them. No wisdom of the wise can find out God; no words of the God-loving can reveal him. The simplicity of the whole natural relation is too deep for the philosopher. The Son alone can reveal God; the child alone understand him. The elder brother companies with the younger, and makes him yet more a child like himself. He interpenetrates his willing companion with his obedient glory. He lets him see how he delights in his father, and lets him know that God is his father too. He rouses in his little brother the sense of their father's will; and the younger, as he hears and obeys, begins to see that his elder brother must be the very image of their father. He becomes more and more of a child, and more and more the Son reveals to him the Father. For he knows that to know the Father is the one thing needful to every child of the Father, the one thing to fill the divine gulf of his necessity. To see the Father is the cry of every child-heart in the universe of the Father—is the need, where not the cry, of every living soul. Comfort yourselves then, brothers and sisters; he to whom the Son will reveal him shall know the Father; and the Son came to us that he might reveal him. 'Eternal Brother,' we cry, 'show us the Father. Be thyself to us, that in thee we may know him. We too are his children: let the other children share with thee in the things of the Father.'

Having spoken to his father first, and now to his disciples, the Lord turns to the whole world, and lets his heart overflow:—St Matthew alone has saved for us the eternal cry:—'Come unto me all ye that labour and are heavy laden, and I will give you rest.'—'I know the Father; come then to me, all ye that labour and are heavy laden.' He does not here call those who want to know the Father; his cry goes far beyond them; it reaches to the ends of the earth. He calls those who are weary; those who do not know that ignorance of the Father is the cause of all their labour and the heaviness of their burden. 'Come unto me,' he says, 'and I will give you rest.'

This is the Lord's own form of his gospel, more intensely personal and direct, at the same time of yet wider inclusion, than that which, at Nazareth, he appropriated from Isaiah; differing from it also in this, that it is interfused with strongest persuasion to the troubled to enter into and share his own eternal rest. I will turn his argument a little. 'I have rest because I know the Father. Be meek and lowly of heart toward him as I am; let him lay his yoke upon you as he lays it on me. I do his will, not my own. Take on you the yoke that I wear; be his child like me; become a babe to whom he can reveal his wonders. Then shall you too find rest to your souls; you shall have the same peace I have; you will be weary and heavy laden no more. I find my yoke easy, my burden light.'

We must not imagine that, when the Lord says, 'Take my yoke upon you,' he means a yoke which he lays on those that come to him; 'my yoke' is the yoke he wears himself, the yoke his father lays upon him, the yoke out of which, that same moment, he speaks, bearing it with glad patience. 'You must take on you the yoke I have taken: the Father lays it upon us.'

The best of the good wine remains; I have kept it to the last. A friend pointed out to me that the Master does not mean we must take on us a yoke like his; we must take on us the very yoke he is carrying.

Dante, describing how, on the first terrace of Purgatory, he walked stooping, to be on a level with Oderisi, who went bowed to the ground by the ponderous burden of the pride he had cherished on earth, says—'I went walking with this heavy-laden soul, just as oxen walk in the yoke': this picture almost always comes to me with the words of the Lord, 'Take my yoke upon you, and learn of me.' Their intent is, 'Take the other end of my yoke, doing as I do, being as I am.' Think of it a moment:—to walk in the same yoke with the Son of Man, doing the same labour with him, and having the same feeling common to him and us! This, and nothing else, is offered the man who would have rest to his soul; is required of the man who would know the Father; is by the Lord pressed upon him to whom he would give the same peace which pervades and sustains his own eternal heart.

But a yoke is for drawing withal: what load is it the Lord is drawing? Wherewith is the cart laden which he would have us help him draw? With what but the will of the eternal, the perfect Father? How should the Father honour the Son, but by giving him his will to embody in deed, by making him hand to his father's heart!—and hardest of all, in bringing home his children! Specially in drawing this load must his yoke-fellow share. How to draw it, he must learn of him who draws by his side.

Whoever, in the commonest duties that fall to him, does as the Father would have him do, bears His yoke along with Jesus; and the Father takes his help for the redemption of the world—for the deliverance of men from the slavery of their own rubbish-laden waggons, into the liberty of God's husbandmen. Bearing the same yoke with Jesus, the man learns to walk step for step with him, drawing, drawing the cart laden with the will of the father of both, and rejoicing with the joy of Jesus. The glory of existence is to take up its burden, and exist for Existence eternal and supreme—for the Father who does his divine and perfect best to impart his glad life to us, making us sharers of that nature which is bliss, and that labour which is peace.

He lives for us; we must live for him. The little ones must take their full share in the great Father's work: his work is the business of the family.

Starts thy soul, trembles thy brain at the thought of such a burden as the will of the eternally creating, eternally saving God? 'How shall mortal man walk in such a yoke,' sayest thou, 'even with the Son of God bearing it also?'

Why, brother, sister, it is the only burden bearable—the only burden that can be borne of mortal! Under any other, the lightest, he must at last sink outworn, his very soul gray with sickness!

He on whom lay the other half of the burden of God, the weight of his creation to redeem, says, 'The yoke I bear is easy; the burden I draw is light'; and this he said, knowing the death he was to die. The yoke did not gall his neck, the burden did not overstrain his sinews, neither did the goal on Calvary fright him from the straight way thither. He had the will of the Father to work out, and that will was his strength as well as his joy. He had the same will as his father. To him the one thing worth living for, was the share the love of his father gave him in his work. He loved his father even to the death of the cross, and eternally beyond it.

When we give ourselves up to the Father as the Son gave himself, we shall not only find our yoke easy and our burden light, but that they communicate ease and lightness; not only will they not make us weary, but they will give us rest from all other weariness. Let us not waste a moment in asking how this can be; the only way to know that, is to take the yoke on us. That rest is a secret for every heart to know, for never a tongue to tell. Only by having it can we know it. If it seem impossible to take the yoke on us, let us attempt the impossible; let us lay hold of the yoke, and bow our heads, and try to get our necks under it. Giving our Father the opportunity, he will help and not fail us. He is helping us every moment, when least we think we need his help; when most we think we do, then may we most boldly, as most earnestly we must, cry for it. What or how much his creatures can do or bear, God only understands; but when most it seems impossible to do or bear, we must be most confident that he will neither demand too much, nor fail with the vital creator-help. That help will be there when wanted—that is, the moment it can be help. To be able beforehand to imagine ourselves doing or bearing, we have neither claim nor need.

It is vain to think that any weariness, however caused, any burden, however slight, may be got rid of otherwise than by bowing the neck to the yoke of the Father's will. There can be no other rest for heart and soul that he has created. From every burden, from every anxiety, from all dread of shame or loss, even loss of love itself, that yoke will set us free.

These words of the Lord—so many as are reported in common by St Matthew and St Luke, namely his thanksgiving, and his statement concerning the mutual knowledge of his father and himself, meet me like a well known face unexpectedly encountered: they come to me like a piece of heavenly bread cut from the gospel of St John. The words are not in that gospel, and in St Matthew's and St Luke's there is nothing more of the kind—in St Mark's nothing like them. The passage seems to me just one solitary flower testifying to the presence in the gospels of Matthew and Luke of the same root of thought and feeling which everywhere blossoms in that of John. It looks as if it had crept out of the fourth gospel into the first and third, and seems a true sign, though no proof, that, however much the fourth be unlike the other gospels, they have all the same origin. Some disciple was able to remember one such word of which the promised comforter brought many to the remembrance of John. I do not see how the more phenomenal gospels are ever to be understood, save through a right perception of the relation in which the Lord stands to his father, which relation is the main subject of the gospel according to St John.

As to the loving cry of the great brother to the whole weary world which Matthew alone has set down, I seem aware of a certain indescribable individuality in its tone, distinguishing it from all his other sayings on record.

Those who come at the call of the Lord, and take the rest he offers them, learning of him, and bearing the yoke of the Father, are the salt of the earth, the light of the world.

## THE SALT AND THE LIGHT OF THE WORLD.

'Ye are the salt of the earth; but if the salt have lost his savour, wherewith shall it be salted? It is thenceforth good for nothing, but to be cast out, and to be trodden under foot of men. Ye are the light of the world. A city that is set on an hill, cannot be hid. Neither do men light a candle, and put it under a bushel, but on a candlestick, and it giveth light unto all that are in the house. Let your light so shine before men, that they may see your good works, and glorify your father which is in heaven.'— *Matthew* v. 3—16.

The Lord knew these men, and had their hearts in his hand; else would he have told them they were the salt of the earth and the light of the world? They were in danger, it is true, of pluming themselves on what he had said of them, of taking their importance to their own credit, and seeing themselves other than God saw them. Yet the Lord does not hesitate to call his few humble disciples the salt of the earth; and every century since has borne witness that such indeed they were—that he spoke of them but the simple fact. Where would the world be now but for their salt and their light! The world that knows neither their salt nor their light may imagine itself now at least greatly retarded by the long-drawn survival of their influences; but such as have chosen aspiration and not ambition, will cry, But for those men, whither should we at this moment be bound! Their Master set them to be salt against corruption, and light against darkness; and our souls answer and say, Lord, they have been the salt, they have been the light of the world!

No sooner has he used the symbol of the salt, than the Lord proceeds to supplement its incompleteness. They were salt which must remember that it is salt; which must live salt, and choose salt, and be salt. For the whole worth of salt lies in its being salt; and all the saltness of the moral salt lies in the will to be salt. To lose its saltness, then, is to cease to exist, save as a vile thing whose very being is unjustifiable. What is to be done with saltless salt!—with such as would teach religion, and know not God!

Having thus carried the figure as far as it will serve him, the Master changes it for another, which he can carry farther. For salt only preserves from growing bad; it does not cause anything to grow better. His disciples are the salt of the world, but they are more. Therefore, having warned the human salt to look to itself that it be indeed salt, he proceeds: 'Ye are the light of the world, a city, a candle,' and so resumes his former path of persuasion and enforcement: 'It is so, therefore make it so.'—'Ye are the salt of the earth; therefore be salt.'—'Ye are the light of the world; therefore shine.'—'Ye are a city; be seen upon your hill.'—'Ye are the Lord's candles; let no bushels cover you. Let your light shine.' Every disciple of the Lord must be a preacher of righteousness.

Cities are the best lighted portions of the world; and perhaps the Lord meant, 'You are a live city, therefore light up your city.' Some connection of the city with light seems probably in his thought, seeing the allusion to the city on the hill comes in the midst of what he says about light in relation to his disciples as the light of the world. Anyhow the city is the best circle in which, and the best centre from which to diffuse moral light. A man brooding in the desert may find the very light of light, but he must go to the city to let it shine.

From the general idea of light, however, associated with the city as visible to all the country around, the Lord turns at once, in this probably fragmentary representation of his words, to the homelier, the more individual and personally applicable figure of the lamp: 'Neither do men light a lamp, and put it under a bushel, but on a lampstand, and it giveth light to all that are in the house,'

Here let us meditate a moment. For what is a lamp or a man lighted? For them that need light, therefore for all. A candle is not lighted for itself; neither is a man. The light that serves self only, is no true light; its one virtue is that it will soon go out. The bushel needs to be lighted, but not by being put over the lamp. The man's own soul needs to be lighted, but light for itself only, light covered by the bushel, is darkness whether to soul or bushel. Light unshared is darkness. To be light indeed, it must shine out. It is of the very essence of light, that it is for others. The thing is true of the spiritual as of the physical light—of the truth as of its type.

The lights of the world are live lights. The lamp that the Lord kindles is a lamp that can will to shine, a soul that must shine. Its true relation to the spirits around it—to God and its fellows, is its light. Then only does it fully shine, when its love, which is its light, shows it to all the souls within its scope, and all those souls to each other, and so does its part to bring all together toward one. In the darkness each soul is alone; in the light the souls are a family. Men do not light a lamp to kill it with a bushel, but to set it on a stand, that it may give light to all that are in the house. The Lord seems to say, 'So have I lighted you, not that you may shine for yourselves, but that you may give light unto all. I have set you like a city on a hill, that the whole earth may see and share in your light. Shine therefore; so shine before men, that they may see your good things and glorify your father for the light with which he has lighted you. Take heed to your light that it be such, that it so shine, that in you men may see the Father—may see your works so good, so plainly his, that they recognize his presence in you, and thank him for you.' There was the danger always of the shadow of the self-bushel clouding the lamp the Father had lighted; and the moment they ceased to show the Father, the light that was in them was darkness. God alone is the light, and our light is the shining of his will in our lives. If our light shine at all, it must be, it can be only in showing the Father; nothing is light that does not bear him witness. The man that sees the glory of God, would turn sick at the thought of glorifying his own self, whose one only possible glory is to shine with the glory of God. When a man tries to shine from the self that is not one with God and filled with his light, he is but making ready for his own gathering contempt. The man who, like his Lord, seeks not his own, but the will of him who sent him, he alone shines. He who would shine in the praises of men, will, sooner or later, find himself but a Gideon's-pitcher left broken on the field.

Let us bestir ourselves then to keep this word of the Lord; and to this end inquire how we are to let our light shine.

To the man who does not try to order his thoughts and feelings and judgments after the will of the Father, I have nothing to say; he can have no light to let shine. For to let our light shine is to see that in every, even the smallest thing, our lives and actions correspond to what we know of God; that, as the true children of our father in heaven, we do everything as he would have us do it. Need I say that to let our light shine is to be just, honourable, true, courteous, more careful over the claim of our neighbour than our own, as knowing ourselves in danger of overlooking it, and not bound to insist on every claim of our own! The man who takes no count of what is fair, friendly, pure, unselfish, lovely, gracious,—where is his claim to call Jesus his master? where his claim to Christianity? What saves his claim from being merest mockery?

The outshining of any human light must be obedience to truth recognized as such; our first show of light as the Lord's disciples must be in doing the things he tells us. Naturally thus we declare him our master, the ruler of our conduct, the enlightener of our souls; and while in the doing of his will a man is learning the loveliness of righteousness, he can hardly fail to let some light shine across the dust of his failures, the exhalations from his faults. Thus will his disciples shine as lights in the world, holding forth the Word of life.

To shine, we must keep in his light, sunning our souls in it by thinking of what he said and did, and would have us think and do. So shall we drink the light like some diamonds, keep it, and shine in the dark. Doing his will, men will see in us that we count the world his, hold that his will and not ours must be done in it. Our very faces will then shine with the hope of seeing him, and being taken home where he is. Only let us remember that trying to look what we ought to be, is the beginning of hypocrisy.

If we do indeed expect better things to come, we must let our hope appear. A Christian who looks gloomy at the mention of death, still more, one who talks of his friends as if he had lost them, turns the bushel of his little-faith over the lamp of the Lord's light. Death is but our visible horizon, and our look ought always to be focussed beyond it. We should never talk as if death were the end of anything.

To let our light shine, we must take care that we have no respect for riches: if we have none, there is no fear of our showing any. To treat the poor man with less attention or cordiality than the rich, is to show ourselves the servants of Mammon. In like manner we must lay no value on the praise of men, or in any way seek it. We must honour no man because of intellect, fame, or success. We must not shrink, in fear of the judgment of men, from doing openly what we hold right; or at all acknowledge as a law-giver what calls itself Society, or harbour the least anxiety for its approval.

In business, the custom of the trade must be understood by both contracting parties, else it can have no place, either as law or excuse, with the disciple of Jesus. The man to whom business is one thing and religion another, is not a disciple. If he refuses to harmonize them by making his business religion, he has already chosen Mammon; if he thinks not to settle the question, it is settled. The most futile of all human endeavours is, to serve God and Mammon. The man who makes the endeavour, betrays his Master in the temple and kisses him in the garden; takes advantage of him in the shop, and offers him 'divine service!' on Sunday. His very church-going is but a further service of Mammon! But let us waste no strength in despising such men; let us rather turn the light upon ourselves: are we not in some way denying him? Is our light bearing witness? Is it shining before men so that they glorify God for it? If it does not shine, it is darkness. In the darkness which a man takes for light, he will thrust at the heart of the Lord himself.

He who goes about his everyday duty as the work the Father has given him to do, is he who lets his light shine. But such a man will not be content with this: he must yet let his light shine. Whatever makes his heart glad, he will have his neighbour share. The body is a lantern; it must not be a dark lantern; the glowing heart must show in the shining face. His glad thought may not be one to impart to his neighbour, but he must not quench the vibration of its gladness ere it reach him. What shall we say of him who comes from his closet, his mountain-top, with such a veil over his face as masks his very humanity? Is it with the Father that man has had communion, whose every movement is self-hampered, and in whose eyes dwell no smiles for the people of his house? The man who receives the quiet attentions, the divine ministrations, of wife or son or daughter, without token of pleasure, without sign of gratitude, can hardly have been with Jesus. Or can he have been with him, and have left him behind in his closet? If his faith in God take from a man his cheerfulness, how shall the face of a man ever shine? And why are they always glad before the face of the Father in heaven? It is true that pain or inward grief may blameless banish all smiling, but even heaviness of heart has no right so to tumble the bushel over the lamp that no ray can get out to tell that love is yet burning within. The man must at least let his dear ones know that something else than displeasure with them is the cause of his clouded countenance.

What a sweet colour the divine light takes to itself in courtesy, whose perfection is the recognition of every man as a temple of the living God. Sorely ruined, sadly defiled the temple may be, but if God had left it, it would be a heap and not a house.

Next to love, specially will the light shine out in fairness. What light can he have in him who is always on his own side, and will never descry reason or right on that of his adversary? And certainly, if he that showeth mercy, as well he that showeth justice, ought to do it with cheerfulness.

But if all our light shine out, and none of our darkness, shall we not be in utmost danger of hypocrisy? Yes, if we but hide our darkness, and do not strive to slay it with our light: what way have we to show it, while struggling to destroy it? Only when we cherish evil, is there hypocrisy in hiding it. A man who is honestly fighting it and showing it no quarter, is already conqueror in Christ, or will soon be—and more than innocent. But our good feelings, those that make for righteousness and unity, we ought to let shine; they claim to commune with the light in others. Many parents hold words unsaid which would lift hundred-weights from the hearts of their children, yea, make them leap for joy. A stern father and a silent mother make mournful, or, which is far worse, hard children. Need I add that, if any one, hearing the injunction to let his light shine, makes himself shine instead, it is because the light is not in him!

But what shall I say of such as, in the name of religion, let only their darkness out—the darkness of worshipped opinion, the darkness of lip-honour and disobedience! Such are those who tear asunder the body of Christ with the explosives of dispute, on the plea of such a unity as alone they can understand, namely a paltry uniformity. What have not the 'good church-man' and the 'strong dissenter' to answer for, who, hiding what true light they have, if indeed they have any, each under the bushel of his party-spirit, radiate only repulsion! There is no schism, none whatever, in using diverse forms of thought or worship: true honesty is never schismatic. The real schismatic is the man who turns away love and justice from the neighbour who holds theories in religious philosophy, or as to church-constitution, different from his own; who denies or avoids his brother because he follows not with him; who calls him a schismatic because he prefers this or that mode of public worship not his. The other *may* be schismatic; he himself certainly *is*. He walks in the darkness of opinion, not in the light of life, not in the faith which worketh by love. Worst of all is division in the name of Christ who came to make one. Neither Paul nor Apollos nor Cephas would—least of all will Christ be the leader of any party save that of his own elect, the party of love—of love which suffereth long and is kind; which envieth not, is not puffed up, doth not behave itself unseemly, seeketh not its own, is not easily provoked, thinketh no evil, rejoiceth not in iniquity, but rejoiceth in the truth, beareth all things, believeth all things, hopeth all things, endureth all things.

'Let your light shine,' says the Lord:—if I have none, the call cannot apply to me; but I must bethink me, lest, in the night I am cherishing about me, the Lord come upon me like a thief. There may be those, however, and I think they are numerous, who, having some, or imagining they have much light, yet have not enough to know the duty of letting it shine on their neighbours. The Lord would have his men so alive with his light, that it should for ever go flashing from each to all, and all, with eternal response, keep glorifying the Father. Dost thou look for a good time coming, friend, when thou shalt know as thou art known? Let the joy of thy hope stream forth upon thy neighbours. Fold them round in that which maketh thyself glad. Let thy nature grow more expansive and communicative. Look like the man thou art—a man who knows something very good. Thou believest thyself on the way to the heart of things: walk so, shine so, that all that see thee shall want to go with thee.

What light issues from such as make their faces long at the very name of death, and look and speak as if it were the end of all things and the worst of evils? Jesus told his men not to fear death; told them his friends should go to be with him; told them they should live in the house of his father and their father; and since then he has risen himself from the tomb, and gone to prepare a place for them: who, what are these miserable refusers of comfort? Not Christians, surely! Oh, yes, they are Christians! 'They are gone,' they say, 'to be for ever with the Lord;' and then they weep and lament, and seem more afraid of starting to join them than of aught else under the sun! To the last attainable moment they cling to what they call life. They are children—were there ever any other such children?—who hang crying to the skirts of their mother, and will not be lifted to her bosom. They are not of Paul's mind: to be with Him is not better! They worship their physician; and their prayer to the God of their life is to spare them from more life. What sort of Christians are they? Where shines their light? Alas for thee, poor world, hadst thou no better lights than these!

You who have light, show yourselves the sons and daughters of Light, of God, of Hope—the heirs of a great completeness. Freely let your light shine.

Only take heed that ye do not your righteousness before men, to be seen of them.

### THE RIGHT HAND AND THE LEFT.

Take heed that ye do not your righteousness before men to be seen of them; otherwise ye have no reward of your father which is in heaven.... But when thou doest alms, let not thy left hand know what thy right hand doeth; that thine alms may be in secret; and thy father which seeth in secret, himself shall reward thee.—- *Matthew* vi. I,3.

Let your light out freely, that men may see it, but not that men may see you. If I do anything, not because it has to be done, not because God would have it so, not that I may do right, not because it is honest, not that I love the thing, not that I may be true to my Lord, not that the truth may be recognized as truth and as his, but that I may be seen as the doer, that I may be praised of men, that I may gain repute or fame; be the thing itself ever so good, I may look to men for my reward, for there is none for me with the Father. If, that light being my pleasure, I do it that the light may shine, and that men may know *the* Light, the father of lights, I do well; but if I do it that I may be seen shining, that the light may be noted as emanating from me and not from another, then am I of those that seek glory of men, and worship Satan; the light that through me may possibly illuminate others, will, in me and for me, be darkness.

*But when thou doest alms, let not thy left hand know what thy right hand doeth.*

How, then, am I to let my light shine, if I take pains to hide what I do?

The injunction is not to hide what you do from others, but to hide it from yourself. The Master would have you not plume yourself upon it, not cherish the thought that you have done it, or confer with yourself in satisfaction over it. You must not count it to your praise. A man must not desire to be satisfied with himself. His right hand must not seek the praise of his left hand. His doing must not invite his after-thinking. The right hand must let the thing done go, as a thing done-with. We must meditate nothing either as a fine thing for us to do, or a fine thing for us to have done. We must not imagine any merit in us: it would be to love a lie, for we can have none; there is no such thing possible. Is there anything to be proud of in refusing to worship the devil? Is it a grand thing, is it a meritorious thing, not to be vile? When we have done all, we are unprofitable servants. Our very best is but decent. What more could it be? Why then think of it as anything more? What things could we or any one do, worthy of being brooded over as possessions. Good to do, they were; bad to pride ourselves upon, they are. Why should a man meditate with satisfaction on having denied himself some selfish indulgence, any more than on having washed his hands? May we roll the rejection of a villainy as a sweet morsel under our tongues? They were the worst villains of all who could be proud of not having committed a villainy; and their pride would but render them the more capable of the villainy, when next the temptation to it came. Even if our supposed merit were of the positive order, and we did every duty perfectly, the moment we began to pride ourselves upon the fact, we should drop into a hell of worthlessness. What are we for but to do our duty? We must do it, and think nothing of ourselves for that, neither care what men think of us for anything. With the praise or blame of men we have nought to do. Their blame may be a good thing, their praise cannot be. But the worst sort of the praise of men is the praise we give ourselves. We must do nothing to be seen of ourselves. We must seek no approbation even, but that of God, else we shut the door of the kingdom from the outside. His approbation will but quicken our sense of unworthiness. What! seek the praise of men for being fair to our own brothers and sisters? What! seek the praise of God for laying our hearts at the feet of him to whom we utterly belong? There is no pride so mean—and all pride is absolutely, essentially mean—as the pride of being holier than our fellow, except the pride of being holy. Such imagined holiness is foulness. Religion itself in the hearts of the unreal, is a dead thing; what seems life in it, is the vermiculate life of a corpse.

There is one word in the context, as we have it in the authorized version, that used to trouble me, seeming to make its publicity a portion of the reward for doing certain right things in secret: I mean the word *openly*, at the ends of the fourth, the sixth, and the eighteenth verses, making the Lord seem to say, 'Avoid the praise of men, and thou shalt at length have the praise of men.'—'Thy father, which seeth in secret, shall reward thee openly.' *Thy reward shall be seen of men! and thou seen as the receiver of the reward!* In what other way could the word, then or now, be fairly understood? It must be the interpolation of some Jew scribe, who, even after learning a little of the Christ, continued unable to conceive as reward anything that did not draw part at least of its sweetness from the gazing eyes of the multitude. Glad was I to find that the word is not in the best manuscripts; and God be thanked that it is left out in the revised version. What shall we think of the daring that could interpolate it! But of like sort is the daring of much exposition of the Master's words. What men have not faith enough to receive, they will still dilute to the standard of their own faculty of reception. If any one say, 'Why did the Lord let the word remain there so long, if he never said it?' I answer: Perhaps that the minds of his disciples might be troubled at its presence, arise against it, and do him right by casting it out—and so Wisdom be justified of her children.

But there are some who, if the notion of reward is not naturally a trouble to them, yet have come to feel it such, because of the words of certain objectors who think to take a higher stand than the Christian, saying the idea of reward for doing right is a low, an unworthy idea. Now, verily, it would be a low thing for any child to do his father's will in the hope that his father would reward him for it; but it is quite another thing for a father whose child endeavours to please him, to let him know that he recognizes his childness toward him, and will be fatherly good to him. What kind of a father were the man who, because there could be no merit or desert in doing well, would not give his child a smile or a pleased word when he saw him trying his best? Would not such acknowledgment from the father be the natural correlate of the child's behaviour? and what would the father's smile be but the perfect reward of the child? Suppose the father to love the child so that he wants to give him everything, but dares not until his character is developed: must he not be glad, and show his gladness, at every shade of a progress that will at length set him free to throne his son over all that he has? 'I am an unprofitable servant,' says the man who has done his duty; but his lord, coming unexpectedly, and finding him at his post, girds himself, and makes him sit down to meat, and comes forth and serves him. How could the divine order of things, founded for growth and gradual betterment, hold and proceed without the notion of return for a thing done? Must there be only current and no tide? How can we be workers with God at his work, and he never say 'Thank you, my child'? Will he take joy in his success and give none? Is he the husbandman to take all the profit, and muzzle the mouth of his ox? When a man does work for another, he has his wages for it, and society exists by the dependence of man upon man through work and wages. The devil is not the inventor of this society; he has invented the notion of a certain degradation in work, a still greater in wages; and following this up, has constituted a Society after his own likeness, which despises work, leaves it undone, and so can claim its wages without disgrace.

If you say, 'No one ought to do right for the sake of reward,' I go farther and say, 'No man *can* do right for the sake of reward. A man may do a thing indifferent, he may do a thing wrong, for the sake of reward; but a thing in itself right, done for reward, would, in the very doing, cease to be right.' At the same time, if a man does right, he cannot escape being rewarded for it; and to refuse the reward, would be to refuse life, and foil the creative love. The whole question is of the kind of reward expected. What first reward for doing well, may I look for? To grow purer in heart, and stronger in the hope of at length seeing God. If a man be not after this fashion rewarded, he must perish. As to happiness or any lower rewards that naturally follow the first—is God to destroy the law of his universe, the divine sequence of cause and effect in order to say: 'You must do well, but you shall gain no good by it; you must lead a dull joyless existence to all eternity, that lack of delight may show you pure'? Could Love create with such end in view? Righteousness does not demand creation; it is Love, not Righteousness, that cannot live alone. The creature must already be, ere Righteousness can put in a claim. But, hearts and souls there, Love itself, which created for love and joy, presses the demand of Righteousness first.

A righteousness that created misery in order to up-hold itself, would be a righteousness that was unrighteous. God will die for righteousness, but never create for a joyless righteousness. To call into being the necessarily and hopelessly incomplete, would be to wrong creation in its very essence. To create for the knowledge of himself, and then not give himself, would be injustice even to cruelty; and if God give himself, what other reward—there can be no *further*—is not included, seeing he is Life and all her children—the All in all? It will take the utmost joy God can give, to let men know him; and what man, knowing him, would mind losing every other joy? Only what other joy could keep from entering, where the God of joy already dwelt? The law of the universe holds, and will hold, the name of the Father be praised:—'Whatsoever a man soweth, that shall he also reap.' 'They have sown the wind, and they shall reap the whirlwind.' 'He that soweth to his flesh, shall of the flesh reap corruption; but he that soweth to the spirit, shall of the spirit reap life everlasting.' 'Whosoever hath, to him shall be given, and he shall have more abundance; but whosoever hath not, from him shall be taken away even that he hath.'

To object to Christianity as selfish, is utter foolishness; Christianity alone gives any hope of deliverance from selfishness. Is it selfish to desire to love? Is it selfish to hope for purity and the sight of God? What better can we do for our neighbour than to become altogether righteous toward him? Will he not be the nearer sharing in the exceeding great reward of a return to the divine idea?

Where is the evil toward God, where the wrong to my neighbour, if I think sometimes of the joys to follow in the train of perfect loving? Is not the atmosphere of God, love itself, the very breath of the Father, wherein can float no thinnest pollution of selfishness, the only material wherewithal to build the airy castles of heaven? 'Creator,' the childlike heart might cry, 'give me all the wages, all the reward thy perfect father-heart can give thy unmeriting child. My fit wages may be pain, sorrow, humiliation of soul: I stretch out my hands to receive them. Thy reward will be to lift me out of the mire of self-love, and bring me nearer to thyself and thy children: welcome, divinest of good things! Thy highest reward is thy purest gift; thou didst make me for it from the first; thou, the eternal life, hast been labouring still to fit me for receiving it—the vision, the knowledge, the possession of thyself. I can seek but what thou waitest and watchest to give: I would be such into whom thy love can flow.'

It seems to me that the only merit that could live before God, is the merit of Jesus—who of himself, at once, untaught, unimplored, laid himself aside, and turned to the Father, refusing his life save in the Father. Like God, of himself he chose righteousness, and so merited to sit on the throne of God. In the same spirit he gave himself afterward to his father's children, and merited the power to transfuse the life-redeeming energy of his spirit into theirs: made perfect, he became the author of eternal salvation unto all them that obey him. But it is a word of little daring, that Jesus had no thought of merit in what he did—that he saw only what he had to be, what he must do.—I speak after the poor fashion of a man lost in what is too great for him, yet is his very life.—Where can be a man's merit in refusing to go down to an abyss of loss—loss of the right to be, loss of his father, loss of himself? Would Satan, with all the instincts and impulses of his origin in him, have *merited* eternal life by refusing to be a devil? Not the less would he have had eternal life; not the less would he have been wrapt in the love and confidence of the Father. He would have had his reward. I cannot imagine thing created meriting aught save by divine courtesy.

I suspect the notion of merit belongs to a low development, and the higher a man rises, the less will he find it worth a thought. Perhaps we shall come to see that it owes what being it has, to man, that it is a thing thinkable only by man. I suspect it is not a thought of the eternal mind, and has in itself no existence, being to God merely a thing thought by man.

> For merit lives from man to man,
> And not from man, O Lord, to thee.

The man, then, who does right, and seeks no praise from men, while he merits nothing, shall be rewarded by his Father, and his reward will be right precious to him.

We must let our light shine, make our faith, our hope, our love, manifest—that men may praise, not us for shining, but the Father for creating the light. No man with faith, hope, love, alive in his soul, could make the divine possessions a show to gain for himself the admiration of men: not the less must they appear in our words, in our looks, in our carriage—above all, in honourable, unselfish, hospitable, helpful deeds. Our light must shine in cheerfulness, in joy, yea, where a man has the gift, in merriment; in freedom from care save for one another, in interest in the things of others, in fearlessness and tenderness, in courtesy and graciousness. In our anger and indignation, specially, must our light shine. But we must give no quarter to the most shadowy thought of how this or that will look. From the faintest thought of the praise of men, we must turn away. No man can be the disciple of Christ and desire fame. To desire fame is ignoble; it is a beggarly greed. In the noble mind, it is the more of an infirmity. There is no aspiration in it—nothing but ambition. It is simply selfishness that would be proud if it could. Fame is the applause of the many, and the judgment of the many is foolish; therefore the greater the fame, the more is the foolishness that swells it, and the worse is the foolishness that longs after it. Aspiration is the sole escape from ambition. He who aspires—that is, does his endeavour to rise above himself—neither lusts to be higher than his neighbour, nor seeks to mount in his opinion. What light there is in him shines the more that he does nothing to be seen of men. He stands in the mist between the gulf and the glory, and looks upward. He loves not his own soul, but longs to be clean.

Out of the gulf into the glory,
  Father, my soul cries out to be lifted.
Dark is the woof of my dismal story,
  Thorough thy sun-warp stormily drifted!—
Out of the gulf into the glory,
Lift me, and save my story.

I have done many things merely shameful;
  I am a man ashamed, my father!
My life is ashamed and broken and blameful—
  The broken and blameful, oh, cleanse and gather!
Heartily shame me, Lord, of the shameful!
To my judge I flee with my blameful.

Saviour, at peace in thy perfect purity,
  Think what it is, not to be pure!
Strong in thy love's essential security,
  Think upon those who are never secure.
Full fill my soul with the light of thy purity;
Fold me in love's security.

O Father, O Brother, my heart is sore aching
  Help it to ache as much as is needful;
Is it you cleansing me, mending, remaking,
  Dear potter-hands, so tender and heedful?
Sick of my past, of my own self aching—
Hurt on, dear hands, with your making.

Proud of the form thou hadst given thy vessel,
  Proud of myself, I forgot my donor;
Down in the dust I began to nestle,
  Poured thee no wine, and drank deep of dishonour!
Lord, thou hast broken, thou mendest thy vessel!
In the dust of thy glory I nestle.

O Lord, the earnest expectation of thy creature waiteth for the manifestation of the sons of God.

## THE HOPE OF THE UNIVERSE.

*Very Good ↓ incredible new thoughts*

For the earnest expectation of the creature waiteth for the manifestation of the sons of God.—*Romans* viii. 19.

Let us try, through these words, to get at the idea in St Paul's mind for which they stand, and have so long stood. It can be no worthless idea they represent—no mere platitude, which a man, failing to understand it at once, may without loss leave behind him. The words mean something which Paul believes vitally associated with the life and death of his Master. He had seen Jesus with his bodily eyes, I think, but he had not seen him with those alone; he had seen and saw him with the real eyes, the eyes that do not see except they understand; and the sight of him had uplifted his whole nature—first his pure will for righteousness, and then his hoping imagination; and out of these, in the knowledge of Jesus, he spoke.

The letters he has left behind him, written in the power of this uplifting, have waked but poor ideas in poor minds; for words, if they seem to mean anything, must always seem to mean something within the scope of the mind hearing them. Words cannot convey the thought of a thinker to a no-thinker; of a largely aspiring and self-discontented soul, to a creature satisfied with his poverty, and counting his meagre faculty the human standard. Neither will they readily reveal the mind of one old in thought, to one who has but lately begun to think. The higher the reader's notion of what St Paul intends—the higher the idea, that is, which his words wake in him, the more likely is it to be the same which moved the man who had seen Jesus, and was his own no more. If a man err in his interpretation, it will hardly be by attributing to his words an intent too high.

First then, what does Paul, the slave of Christ, intend by 'the creature' or 'the creation'? If he means the *visible world*, he did not surely, and without saying so, mean to exclude the noblest part of it—the sentient! If he did, it is doubly strange that he should immediately attribute not merely sense, but conscious sense, to that part, the insentient, namely, which remained. If you say he does so but by a figure of speech, I answer that a figure that meant less than it said—and how much less would not this?—would be one altogether unworthy of the Lord's messenger.

First, I repeat, to exclude the sentient from the term common to both in the word *creation* or *creature*—and then to attribute the capabilities of the sentient to the insentient, as a mere figure to express the hopes of men with regard to the perfecting of the insentient for the comfort of men, were a violence as unfit in rhetoric as in its own nature. Take another part of the same utterance: 'For we know that the whole creation groaneth and travaileth in pain together until now:' is it not manifest that to interpret such words as referring to the mere imperfections of the insensate material world, would be to make of the phrase a worthless hyperbole? I am inclined to believe the apostle regarded the whole visible creation as, in far differing degrees of consciousness, a live outcome from the heart of the living one, who is all and in all: such view, at the same time, I do not care to insist upon; I only care to argue that the word *creature* or *creation* must include everything in creation that has sentient life. That I should in the class include a greater number of phenomena than a reader may be prepared to admit, will nowise affect the force of what I have to say, seeing my point is simply this: that in the term *creation*, Paul comprises all creatures capable of suffering; the condition of which sentient, therefore superior portion, gives him occasion to speak of the whole creation as suffering in the process of its divine evolution or development, groaning and travailing as in the pangs of giving birth to a better self, a nobler world. It is not necessary to the idea that the creation should know what it is groaning after, or wherein the higher condition constituting its deliverance must consist. The human race groans for deliverance: how much does the race know that its redemption lies in becoming one with the Father, and partaking of his glory? Here and there one of the race knows it—which is indeed a pledge for the race—but the race cannot be said to know its own lack, or to have even a far-off notion of what alone can stay its groaning. In like manner the whole creation is groaning after an unforeseen yet essential birth—groans with the necessity of being freed from a state that is but a transitional and not a true one, from a condition that nowise answers to the intent in which existence began. In both the lower creation and the higher, this same groaning of the fettered idea after a freer life, seems the first enforced decree of a holy fate, and itself the first movement of the hampered thing toward the liberty of another birth.

To believe that God made many of the lower creatures merely for prey, or to be the slaves of a slave, and writhe under the tyrannies of a cruel master who will not serve his own master; that he created and is creating an endless succession of them to reap little or no good of life but its cessation—a doctrine held by some, and practically accepted by multitudes—is to believe in a God who, so far as one portion at least of his creation is concerned, is a demon. But a creative demon is an absurdity; and were such a creator possible, he would not be God, but must one day be found and destroyed by the real God. Not the less the fact remains, that miserable suffering abounds among them, and that, even supposing God did not foresee how creation would turn out for them, the thing lies at his door. He has besides made them so far dumb that they cannot move the hearts of the oppressors into whose hands he has given them, telling how hard they find the world, how sore their life in it. The apostle takes up their case, and gives us material for an answer to such as blame God for their sad condition.

There are many, I suspect, who from the eighth chapter of St Paul's epistle to the Romans, gather this much and no more:—that the lower animals alive at the coming of the Lord, whensoever that may be, will thenceforward, with such as thereafter may come into existence, lead a happy life for the time allotted them! Strong champions of God, these profound believers! What lovers of life, what disciples of St Paul, nay, what disciples of Jesus, to whom such a gloss is consolation for the moans of a universe! Truly, the furnace of affliction they would extinguish thus, casts out the more an evil odour! For all the creatures who through ages of misery have groaned and travailed and died, to these mild Christians it is enough that they are dead, therefore, as they would argue, out of it now! 'It is well with them,' I seem to hear such say; 'they are mercifully dealt with; their sufferings are over; they had not to live on for ever in oppression. The God of their life has taken from them their past, and troubles them with no future!' It is true this were no small consolation concerning such as are gone away! Surely rest is better than ceaseless toil and pain! But what shall we say of such a heedless God as those Christians are content to worship! Is he a merciful God? Is he a loving God? How shall he die to escape the remorse of the authorship of so much misery? Our pity turns from the dead creature to the live creator who could live and know himself the maker of so many extinguished hearts, whose friend was—not he, but Death. Blessed be the name of the Father of Jesus, there is no such creator!

Be we have not to do with the dead only; there are those which live and suffer: is there no comfort concerning them, but that they too shall at length die and leave their misery? And what shall we say of those coming, and yet to come and pass—evermore issuing from the fountain of life, daily born into evil things? Will the consolation that they will soon die, suffice for the heart of the child who laments over his dead bird or rabbit, and would fain love that father in heaven who keeps on making the creatures? Alas, they are crowding in; they cannot help themselves; their misery is awaiting them! Would those Christians have me believe in a God who differentiates creatures from himself, only that they may be the prey of other creatures, or spend a few hours or years, helpless and lonely, speechless and without appeal, in merciless hands, then pass away into nothingness? I will not; in the name of Jesus, I will not. Had he not known something better, would he have said what he did about the father of men and the sparrows?

What many men call their beliefs, are but the prejudices they happen to have picked up: why should such believers waste a thought as to how their paltry fellow-inhabitants of the planet fare? Many indeed have all their lives been too busy making their human fellows groan and sweat for their own fancied well-being, to spare a thought for the fate of the yet more helpless. But there are not a few, who would be indignant at having their belief in God questioned, who yet seem greatly to fear imagining him better than he is: whether is it he or themselves they dread injuring by expecting too much of him? 'You see the plain facts of the case!' they say. 'There is no questioning them! What can be done for the poor things—except indeed you take the absurd notion into your head, that they too have a life beyond the grave?'

Why should such a notion seem to you absurd? I answer. The teachers of the nation have unwittingly, it seems to me through unbelief, wronged the animals deeply by their silence anent the thoughtless popular presumption that they have no hereafter; thus leaving them deprived of a great advantage to their position among men. But I suppose they too have taken it for granted that the Preserver of man and beast never had a thought of keeping one beast alive beyond a certain time; in which case heartless men might well argue he did not care how they wronged them, for he meant them no redress. Their immortality is no new faith with me, but as old as my childhood.

Do you believe in immortality for yourself? I would ask any reader who is not in sympathy with my hope for the animals. If not, I have no argument with you. But if you do, why not believe in it for them? Verily, were immortality no greater a thing for the animals than it seems for men to some who yet profess to expect it, I should scarce care to insist upon their share in it. But if the thought be anywise precious to you, is it essential to your enjoyment in it, that nothing less than yourself should share its realization? Are you the lowest kind of creature that *could* be permitted to live? Had God been of like heart with you, would he have given life and immortality to creatures so much less than himself as we? Are these not worth making immortal? How, then, were they worth calling out of the depth of no-being? It is a greater deed, to make be that which was not, than to seal it with an infinite immortality: did God do that which was not worth doing? What he thought worth making, you think not worth continuing made! You would have him go on for ever creating new things with one hand, and annihilating those he had made with the other—for I presume you would not prefer the earth to be without animals! If it were harder for God to make the former go on living, than to send forth new, then his creatures were no better than the toys which a child makes, and destroys as he makes them. For what good, for what divine purpose is the maker of the sparrow present at its death, if he does not care what becomes of it? What is he there for, I repeat, if he have no care that it go well with his bird in its dying, that it be neither comfortless nor lost in the abyss? If his presence be no good to the sparrow, are you very sure what good it will be to you when your hour comes? Believe it is not by a little only that the heart of the universe is tenderer, more loving, more just and fair, than yours or mine.

If you did not believe you were yourself to out-live death, I could not blame you for thinking all was over with the sparrow; but to believe in immortality for yourself, and not care to believe in it for the sparrow, would be simply hard-hearted and selfish. If it would make you happy to think there was life beyond death for the sparrow as well as for yourself, I would gladly help you at least to hope that there may be.

I know of no reason why I should not look for the animals to rise again, in the same sense in which I hope myself to rise again—which is, to reappear, clothed with another and better form of life than before. If the Father will raise his children, why should he not also raise those whom he has taught his little ones to love? Love is the one bond of the universe, the heart of God, the life of his children: if animals can be loved, they are loveable; if they can love, they are yet more plainly loveable: love is eternal; how then should its object perish? Must the very immortality of love divide the bond of love? Must the love live on for ever without its object? or worse still, must the love die with its object, and be eternal no more than it? What a mis-invented correlation in which the one side was eternal, the other, where not yet annihilated, constantly perishing! Is not our love to the animals a precious variety of love? And if God gave the creatures to us, that a new phase of love might be born in us toward another kind of life from the same fountain, why should the new life be more perishing than the new love? Can you imagine that, if, here-after, one of God's little ones were to ask him to give again one of the earth's old loves—kitten, or pony, or squirrel, or dog, which he had taken from him, the Father would say no? If the

77

thing was so good that God made it for and gave it to the child at first who never asked for it, why should he not give it again to the child who prays for it because the Father had made him love it? What a child may ask for, the Father will keep ready.

That there are difficulties in the way of believing thus, I grant; that there are impossibilities, I deny. Perhaps the first difficulty that occurs is, the many forms of life which we cannot desire again to see. But while we would gladly keep the perfected forms of the higher animals, we may hope that those of many other kinds are as transitory as their bodies, belonging but to a stage of development. All animal forms tend to higher: why should not the individual, as well as the race, pass through stages of ascent. If I have myself gone through each of the typical forms of lower life on my way to the human—a supposition by antenatal history rendered probable—and therefore may have passed through any number of individual forms of life, I do not see why each of the lower animals should not as well pass upward through a succession of bettering embodiments. I grant that the theory requires another to complement it; namely, that those men and women, who do not even approximately fulfil the conditions of their elevated rank, who will not endeavour after the great human-divine idea, striving to ascend, are sent away back down to that stage of development, say of fish or insect or reptile, beyond which their moral nature has refused to advance. Who has not seen or known men who *appeared* not to have passed, or indeed in some things to have approached the development of the more human of the lower animals! Let those take care who look contemptuously upon the animals, lest, in misusing one of them, they misuse some ancestor of their own, sent back, as the one mercy for him, to reassume far past forms and conditions—far past in physical, that is, but not in moral development—and so have another opportunity of passing the self-constituted barrier. The suggestion may appear very ridiculous, and no doubt lends itself to humorous comment; but what if it should be true! what if the amused reader should himself be getting ready to follow the remanded ancestor! Upon it, however, I do not care to spend thought or time, least of all argument; what I care to press is the question—If we believe in the progress of creation as hitherto manifested, also in the marvellous changes of form that take place in every individual of certain classes, why should there be any difficulty in hoping that old lives may reappear in new forms? The typical soul reappears in higher formal type; why may not also the individual soul reappear in higher form?

Multitudes evidently count it safest to hold by a dull scheme of things: can it be because, like David in Browning's poem *Saul*, they dread lest they should worst the Giver by inventing better gifts than his? That we do not know, is the best reason for hoping to the full extent God has made possible to us. If then we go wrong, it will be in the direction of the right, and with such aberration as will be easier to correct than what must come of refusing to imagine, and leaving the dullest traditional prepossessions to rule our hearts and minds, with no claim but the poverty of their expectation from the paternal riches. Those that hope little cannot grow much. To them the very glory of God must be a small thing, for their hope of it is so small as not to be worth rejoicing in. That he is a faithful creator means nothing to them for far the larger portion of the creatures he has made! Truly their notion of faithfulness is poor enough; how then can their faith be strong! In the very nature of divine things, the common-place must be false. The stupid, self-satisfied soul, which cannot know its own stupidity, and will not trouble itself either to understand or to imagine, is the farthest behind of all the backward children in God's nursery.

As I say, then, I know no cause of reasonable difficulty in regard to the continued existence of the lower animals, except the present nature of some of them. But what Christian will dare to say that God does not care about them?—and he knows them as we cannot know them. Great or small, they are his. Great are all his results; small are all his beginnings. That we have to send many of his creatures out of this phase of their life because of their hurtfulness in this phase of ours, is to me no stumbling-block. The very fact that this has always had to be done, the long protracted combat of the race with such, and the constantly repeated though not invariable victory of the man, has had an essential and incalculable share in the development of humanity, which is the rendering of man capable of knowing God; and when their part to that end is no longer necessary, changed conditions may speedily so operate that the wolf shall dwell with the lamb, and the leopard lie down with the kid. The difficulty may go for nothing in view of the forces of that future with which this loving speculation concerns itself.

I would now lead my companion a little closer to what the apostle says in the nineteenth verse; to come closer, if we may, to the idea that burned in his heart when he wrote what we call the eighth chapter of his epistle to the Romans. Oh, how far ahead he seems, in his hope for the creation, of the footsore and halting brigade of Christians at present crossing the world! He knew Christ, and could therefore look into the will of the Father.

*For the earnest expectation of the creature waiteth for the manifestation of the sons of God*!

At the head of one of his poems, Henry Vaughan has this Latin translation of the verse: I do not know whether he found or made it, but it is closer to its sense than ours:—

'Etenim res creatae exerto capite observantes expectant revelationem filiorum Dei.'—'For the things created, watching with head thrust out, await the revelation of the sons of God.'

Why?

Because God has subjected the creation to vanity, in the hope that the creation itself shall be delivered from the bondage of corruption into the glorious liberty of the children of God. For this double deliverance—from corruption and the consequent subjection to vanity, the creation is eagerly watching.

The bondage of corruption God encounters and counteracts by subjection to vanity. Corruption is the breaking up of the essential idea; the falling away from the original indwelling and life-causing thought. It is met by the suffering which itself causes. That suffering is for redemption, for deliverance. It is the life in the corrupting thing that makes the suffering possible; it is the live part, not the corrupted part that suffers; it is the redeemable, not the doomed thing, that is subjected to vanity. The race in which evil—that is, corruption, is at work, needs, as the one means for its rescue, subjection to vanity; it is the one hope against the supremacy of corruption; and the whole encircling, harboring, and helping creation must, for the sake of man, its head, and for its own further sake too, share in this subjection to vanity with its hope of deliverance.

Corruption brings in vanity, causes empty aching gaps in vitality. This aching is what most people regard as evil: it is the unpleasant cure of evil. It takes all shapes of suffering—of the body, of the mind, of the heart, of the spirit. It is altogether beneficent: without this ever invading vanity, what hope would there be for the rich and powerful, accustomed to, and set upon their own way? what hope for the self-indulgent, the conceited, the greedy, the miserly? The more things men seek, the more varied the things they imagine they need, the more are they subject to vanity— all the forms of which may be summed in the word disappointment. He who would not house with disappointment, must seek the incorruptible, the true. He must break the bondage of havings and shows; of rumours, and praises, and pretences, and selfish pleasures. He must come out of the false into the real; out of the darkness into the light; out of the bondage of corruption into the glorious liberty of the children of God. To bring men to break with corruption, the gulf of the inane yawns before them. Aghast in soul, they cry, 'Vanity of vanities! all is vanity!' and beyond the abyss begin to espy the eternal world of truth.

Note now 'the hope that the creation itself also,' as something besides and other than God's men and women, 'shall be delivered from the bondage of corruption, into the liberty of the glory of the children of God.' The creation then is to share in the deliverance and liberty and glory of the children of God. Deliverance from corruption, liberty from bondage, must include escape from the very home and goal of corruption, namely death,—and that in all its kinds and degrees. When you say then that for the children of God there is no more death, remember that the deliverance of the creature is from the bondage of corruption into the glorious liberty of the children of God. Dead, in bondage to corruption, how can they share in the liberty of the children of Life? Where is their deliverance?

If such then be the words of the apostle, does he, or does he not, I ask, hold the idea of the immortality of the animals? If you say all he means is, that the creatures alive at the coming of the Lord will be set free from the tyranny of corrupt man, I refer you to what I have already said of the poverty of such an interpretation, accepting the failure of justice and love toward those that have passed away, are passing, and must yet, ere that coming, be born to pass away for ever. For the man whose heart aches to adore a faithful creator, what comfort lies in such good news! He must perish for lack of a true God! Oh lame conclusion to the grand prophecy! Is God a mocker, who will not be mocked? Is there a past to God with which he has done? Is Time too much for him? Is he God enough to care for those that happen to live at one present time, but not God enough to care for those that happened to live at another present time? Or did he care for them, but could not help them? Shall we not rather believe that the vessels of less honour, the misused, the maltreated, shall be filled full with creative wine at last? Shall not the children have little dogs under the Father's table, to which to let fall plenty of crumbs? If there was such provision for the sparrows of our Lord's time of sojourn, and he will bring yet better with him when he comes again, how should the dead sparrows and their sorrows be passed over of him with whom is no variableness, neither shadow of turning? Or would the deliverance of the creatures into the groaned-for liberty have been much worth mentioning, if within a few years their share in the glory of the sons of God was to die away in death? But the gifts of God are without repentance.

How St Paul longs for and loves liberty! Only true lover of liberty is he, who will die to give it to his neighbour! St Paul loved liberty more than his own liberty. But then see how different his notion of the liberty on its way to the children of God, from the dull modern fancies of heaven still set forth in the popular hymn-books! The new heaven and the new earth will at least be a heaven and an earth! What would the newest earth be to the old children without its animals? Barer than the heavens emptied of the constellations that are called by their names. Then, if the earth must have its animals, why not the old ones, already dear? The sons of God are not a new race of sons of God, but the old race glorified:—why a new race of animals, and not the old ones glorified?

The apostle says they are to share in the liberty of the sons of God: will it not then be a liberty like ours, a liberty always ready to be offered on the altar of love? What sweet service will not that of the animals be, thus offered! How sweet also to minister to them in their turns of need! For to us doubtless will they then flee for help in any difficulty, as now they flee from us in dread of our tyranny. What lovelier feature in the newness of the new earth, than the old animals glorified with us, in their home with us—our common home, the house of our father—each kind an unfailing pleasure to the other! Ah, what horses! Ah, what dogs! Ah, what wild beasts, and what birds in the air! The whole redeemed creation goes to make up St Paul's heaven. He had learned of him who would leave no one out; who made the excuse for his murderers that they did not know what they were doing.

Is not the prophecy on the groaning creation to have its fulfilment in the new heavens and the new earth, wherein dwelleth righteousness? Does not this involve its existence beyond what we call this world? Why should it not then involve immortality? Would it not be more like the king eternal, immortal, invisible, to know no life but the immortal? to create nothing that could die; to slay nothing but evil? 'For he is not a God of the dead, but of the living; for all live unto him.'

But what is this liberty of the children of God, for which the whole creation is waiting? The children themselves are waiting for it: when they have it, then will their house and retinue, the creation, whose fate hangs on that of the children, share it with them: what is this liberty?

All liberty must of course consist in the realization of the ideal harmony between the creative will and the created life; in the correspondence of the creature's active being to the creator's idea, which is his substantial soul. In other words the creature's liberty is what his obedience to the law of his existence, the will of his maker, effects for him. The instant a soul moves counter to the will of its prime cause, the universe is its prison; it dashes against the walls of it, and the sweetest of its uplifting and sustaining forces at once become its manacles and fetters. But St Paul is not at the moment thinking either of the metaphysical notion of liberty, or of its religious realization; he has in his thought the birth of the soul's consciousness of freedom.

'And not only so'—that the creation groaneth and travaileth—'but ourselves also, which have the first fruits of the spirit, even we ourselves groan within ourselves, waiting for.... the redemption of our body.'—We are not free, he implies, until our body is redeemed; then all the creation will be free with us. He regards the creation as part of our embodiment. The whole creation is waiting for the manifestation of the sons of God—that is, the redemption of their body, the idea of which extends to their whole material envelopment, with all the life that belongs to it. For this as for them, the bonds of corruption must fall away; it must enter into the same liberty with them, and be that for which it was created—a vital temple, perfected by the unbroken indwelling of its divinity.

The liberty here intended, it may be unnecessary to say, is not that essential liberty—freedom from sin, but the completing of the redemption of the spirit by the redemption of the body, the perfecting of the greater by its necessary complement of the less. Evil has been constantly at work, turning our house of the body into a prison; rendering it more opaque and heavy and insensible; casting about it bands and cerements, and filling it with aches and pains. The freest soul, the purest of lovers, the man most incapable of anything mean, would not, for all his mighty liberty, yet feel absolutely at large while chained to a dying body—nor the less hampered, but the more, that that dying body was his own. The redemption of the body, therefore, the making of it for the man a genuine, perfected, responsive house-alive, is essential to the apostle's notion of a man's deliverance. The new man must have a new body with a new heaven and earth. St Paul never thinks of himself as released from body; he desires a perfect one, and of a nobler sort; he would inhabit a heaven-made house, and give up the earth-made one, suitable only to this lower stage of life, infected and unsafe from the first, and now much dilapidated in the service of the Master who could so easily give him a better. He wants a spiritual body—a body that will not thwart but second the needs and aspirations of the spirit. He had in his mind, I presume, such a body as the Lord died with, changed by the interpenetrating of the creative indwelling will, to a heavenly body, the body with which he rose. A body like the Lord's is, I imagine, necessary to bring us into true and perfect contact with the creation, of which there must be multitudinous phases whereof we cannot now be even aware.

The way in which both good and indifferent people alike lay the blame on their bodies, and look to death rather than God-aided struggle to set them at liberty, appears to me low and cowardly: it is the master fleeing from the slave, despising at once and fearing him. We must hold the supremacy over our bodies, but we must not despise body; it is a divine thing. Body and soul are in the image of God; and the lord of life was last seen in the glorified body of his death. I believe that he still wears that body. But we shall do better without these bodies that suffer and grow old—which may indeed, as some think, be but the outer cases, the husks of our real bodies. Endlessly helpful as they have been to us, and that, in a measure incalculable, through their very subjection to vanity, we are yet surely not in altogether and only helpful company, so long as the houses wherein we live have so many spots and stains in them which friendly death, it may be, can alone wash out— so many weather-eaten and self-engendered sores which the builder's hand, pulling down and rebuilding of fresh and nobler material, alone can banish.

When the sons, then, are free, when their bodies are redeemed, they will lift up with them the lower creation into their liberty. St Paul seems to believe that perfection in their kind awaits also the humbler inhabitants of our world, its advent to follow immediately on the manifestation of the sons of God: for our sakes and their own they have been made subject to vanity; for our sakes and their own they shall be restored and glorified, that is, raised higher with us.

Has the question no interest for you? It would have much, had you now what you must one day have—a heart big enough to love any life God has thought fit to create. Had the Lord cared no more for what of his father's was lower than himself, than you do for what of your father's is lower than you, you would not now be looking for any sort of redemption.

I have omitted in my quotations the word *adoption* used in both English versions: it is no translation of the Greek word for which it stands. It is used by St Paul as meaning the same thing with the phrase, 'the redemption of the body'—a fact to bring the interpretation given it at once into question. Falser translation, if we look at the importance of the thing signified, and its utter loss in the word used to represent it, not to mention the substitution for that of the apostle, of an idea not only untrue but actively mischievous, was never made. The thing St Paul means in the word he uses, has simply nothing to do with adoption—nothing whatever. In the beginning of the fourth chapter of his epistle to the Galatians, he makes perfectly clear what he intends by it. His unusual word means the father's recognition, when he comes of age, of the child's relation to him, by giving him his fitting place of dignity in the house; and here the deliverance of the body is the act of this recognition by the great Father, completing and crowning and declaring the freedom of the man, the perfecting of the last lingering remnant of his deliverance. St Paul's word, I repeat, has nothing to do with *adoption*; it means the manifestation of the grown-up sons of God; the showing of those as sons, who have always been his children; the bringing of them out before the universe in such suitable attire and with such fit attendance, that to look at them is to see what they are, the sons of the house—such to whom their elder brother applied the words: 'I said ye are Gods.'

If then the sons groan within themselves, looking to be lifted up, and the other inhabitants of the same world groan with them and cry, shall they not also be lifted up? Have they not also a faithful creator? He must be a selfish man indeed who does not desire that it should be so.

It appears then, that, in the expectation of the apostle, the new heavens and the new earth in which dwell the sons of God, are to be inhabited by blessed animals also—inferior, but risen—and I think, yet to rise in continuous development.

Here let me revert a moment, and say a little more clearly and strongly a thing I have already said:—

When the apostle speaks of the whole creation, is it possible he should have dismissed the animals from his thoughts, to regard the trees and flowers bearing their part in the groaning and travailing of the sore burdened world? Or could he, animals and trees and flowers forgotten, have intended by the creation that groaned and travailed, only the bulk of the earth, its mountains and valleys, plains and seas and rivers, its agglomeration of hard and soft, of hot and cold, of moist and dry? If he could, then the portion that least can be supposed to feel or know, is regarded by the apostle of love as immeasurably more important than the portion that loves and moans and cries. Nor is this all; for thereupon he attributes the suffering-faculty of the excluded, far more sentient portion at least, to the altogether inferior and less sentient, and upon the ground of that faculty builds the vision of its redemption! If it could be so, then how should the seeming apostle's affected rhapsody of hope be to us other than a mere puff-ball of falsest rhetoric, a special-pleading for nothing, as degrading to art as objectless in nature?

Much would I like to know clearly what animals the apostle saw on his travels, or around his home when he had one—their conditions, and their relations to their superiors. Anyhow they were often suffering creatures; and Paul was a man growing hourly in likeness to his maker and theirs, therefore overflowing with sympathy. Perhaps as he wrote, there passed through his mind a throb of pity for the beasts he had to kill at Ephesus.

If the Lord said very little about animals, could he have done more for them than tell men that his father cared for them? He has thereby wakened and is wakening in the hearts of men a seed his father planted. It grows but slowly, yet has already borne a little precious fruit. His loving friend St Francis has helped him, and many others have tried, and are now trying to help him: whoever sows the seed of that seed the Father planted is helping the Son. Our behaviour to the animals, our words concerning them, are seed, either good or bad, in the hearts of our children. No one can tell to what the animals might not grow, even here on the old earth under the old heaven, if they were but dealt with according to their true position in regard to us. They are, in sense very real and divine, our kindred. If I call them our poor relations, it is to suggest that poor relations are often ill used. Relatives, poor or rich, may be such ill behaved, self-assertive, disagreeable persons, that we cannot treat them as we gladly would; but our endeavour should be to develop every true relation. He who is prejudiced against a relative because he is poor, is himself an ill-bred relative, and to be ill-bred is an excluding fault with the court of the high countries. There, poverty is welcome, vulgarity inadmissible.

Those who love certain animals selfishly, pampering them, as so many mothers do their children with worse results, that they may be loved of them in return, betray them to their enemies. They are not lovers of animals, but only of favourites, and do their part to make the rest of the world dislike animals. Theirs are the dogs that inhospitably growl and bark and snap, moving the indifferent to dislike, and confirming the unfriendly in their antagonism. Any dog-parliament, met in the interests of their kind, would condemn such dogs to be discreetly bitten, and their mistresses to be avoided. And certainly, if animals are intended to live and grow, she is the enemy of any individual animal, who stunts his moral and intellectual development by unwise indulgence. Of whatever nature be the heaven of the animals, that animal is not in the fair way to enter it. The education of the lower lies at the door of the higher, and in true education is truest kindness.

But what shall I say of such as for any kind of end subject animals to torture? I dare hardly trust myself to the expression of my judgment of their conduct in this regard.

'We are investigators; we are not doing it for our own sakes, but for the sake of others, our fellow-men.'

The higher your motive for it, the greater is the blame of your unrighteousness. Must we congratulate you on such a love for your fellows as inspires you to wrong the weaker than they, those that are without helper against you? Shall we count the man worthy who, for the sake of his friend, robbed another man too feeble to protect himself, and too poor to punish his assailant? For the sake of your children, would you waylay a beggar? No real good can grow in the soil of injustice.

I cannot help suspecting, however, that the desire to know has a greater share in the enormity than the desire to help. Alas for the science that will sacrifice the law of righteousness but to behold a law of sequence! The tree of knowledge will never prove to man the tree of life. There is no law says, Thou shalt know; a thousand laws cry out, Thou shalt do right. These men are a law unto themselves—and what a law! It is the old story: the greed of knowing casts out righteousness, and mercy, and faith. Whatever believed a benefit may or may not thus be wrought for higher creatures, the injustice to the lower is nowise affected. Justice has no respect of persons, but they are surely the weaker that stand more in need of justice!

Labour is a law of the universe, and is not an evil. Death is a law of this world at least, and is not an evil. Torture is the law of no world but the hell of human invention. Labour and death are for the best good of those that labour and die; they are laws of life. Torture is doubtless over-ruled for the good of the tortured, but it will one day burn a very hell in the hearts of the torturers.

Torture can be inflicted only by the superior. The divine idea of a superior, is one who requires duty, and protects, helps, delivers: our relation to the animals is that of their superiors in the family, who require labour, it may be, but are just, helpful, protective. Can they know anything of the Father who neither love nor rule their inferiors, but use them as a child his insensate toys, pulling them to pieces to know what is inside them? Such men, so-called of science—let them have the dignity to the fullness of its worth—lust to know as if a man's life lay in knowing, as if it were a vile thing to be ignorant—so vile that, for the sake of his secret hoard of facts, they do right in breaking with torture into the house of the innocent! Surely they shall not thus find the way of understanding! Surely there is a maniac thirst for knowledge, as a maniac thirst for wine or for blood! He who loves knowledge the most genuinely, will with the most patience wait for it until it can be had righteously.

Need I argue the injustice? Can a sentient creature come forth without rights, without claim to well-being, or to consideration from the other creatures whom they find, equally without action of their own, present in space? If one answer, 'For aught I know, it may be so,'—Where then are thy own rights? I ask. If another have none, thine must lie in thy superior power; and will there not one day come a stronger than thou? Mayst thou not one day be in Naboth's place, with an Ahab getting up to go into thy vineyard to possess it? The rich man may come prowling after thy little ewe lamb, and what wilt thou have to say? He may be the stronger, and thou the weaker! That the rights of the animals are so much less than ours, does not surely argue them the less rights! They have little, and we have much; ought they therefore to have less and we more? Must we not rather be the more honourably anxious that they have their little to the full. Every gain of injustice is a loss to the world; for life consists neither in length of days nor in ease of body. Greed of life and wrong done to secure it, will never work anything but direst loss. As to knowledge, let justice guide thy search and thou wilt know the sooner. Do the will of God, and thou shalt know God, and he will open thine eyes to look into the very heart of knowledge. Force thy violent way, and gain knowledge, to miss truth. Thou mayest wound the heart of God, but thou canst not rend it asunder to find the Truth that sits there enthroned.

What man would he be who accepted the offer to be healed and kept alive by means which necessitated the torture of certain animals? Would he feel himself a gentleman—walking the earth with the sense that his life and conscious well-being were informed and upheld by the agonies of other lives?

'I hope, sir, your health is better than it has been?'

'Thank you, I am wonderfully restored—have entered in truth upon a fresh lease of life. My organism has been nourished with the agonies of several dogs, and the pangs of a multitude of rabbits and guinea-pigs, and I am aware of a marvellous change for the better. They gave me their lives, and I gave them in return worse pains than mine. The bargain has proved a quite satisfactory one! True, their lives were theirs, not mine; but then their sufferings were theirs, not mine! They could not defend themselves; they had not a word to say, so reasonable was the exchange. Poor fools! they were neither so wise, nor so strong, nor such lovers of comfort as I! If they could not take care of themselves, that was their look-out, not mine! Every animal for himself!'

There was a certain patriotic priest who thought it better to put a just man to death than that a whole nation should perish. Precious salvation that might be wrought by injustice! But then the just man taught that the rich man and the beggar must one day change places.

'To set the life of a dog against the life of a human being!'

No, but the torture of a dog against the prolonged life of a being capable of torturing him. Priceless gain, the lengthening of such a life, to the man and his friends and his country!

That the animals do not suffer so much as we should under like inflictions, I hope true, and think true. But is toothache nothing, because there are yet worse pains for head and face?

Not a few who now regard themselves as benefactors of mankind, will one day be looked upon with a disapprobation which no argument will now convince them they deserve. But yet another day is coming, when they will themselves right sorrowfully pour out disapprobation upon their own deeds; for they are not stones but men, and must repent. Let them, in the interests of humanity, give their own entrails to the knife, their own silver cord to be laid bare, their own golden bowl to be watched throbbing, and I will worship at their feet. But shall I admire their discoveries at the expense of the stranger—nay, no stranger—the poor brother within their gates?

Your conscience does not trouble you? Take heed that the light that is in you be not darkness. Whatever judgment mean, will it suffice you in that hour to say, 'My burning desire to know how life wrought in him, drove me through the gates and bars of his living house'? I doubt if you will add, in your heart any more than with your tongue, 'and I did well.'

To those who expect a world to come, I say then, Let us take heed how we carry ourselves to the creation which is to occupy with us the world to come.

To those whose hearts are sore for that creation, I say, The Lord is mindful of his own, and will save both man and beast.

THE END.

Made in the USA